LEST WE

Praying the M

GW01091479

By William G. Storey

Paulist Press
New York and Mahwah

The Publisher gratefully acknowledges the following:
Permission from Charles M. Guilbert, Custodian, *The Book of Common Prayer*, 1977, to reprint four Biblical Canticles and seven Collects.

Permission to reprint the translation of the *Victimae paschali laudes* ("O flock of Christ, your homage bring") © 1969, James Quinn, S.J., printed by permission of Geoffrey Chapman, a division of Cassell Ltd.

Permission to reprint The Rev. Dr. John Webster Grant's translations of the *Veni Creator Spiritus* and the *Veni Sancte Spiritus* from The Hymn Book of the Anglican Church of Canada and the United Church of Canada, © 1971.

Permission to reprint the translation of *Pange lingua gloriosi:* "Hail our Savior's glorious Body" © 1969, James Quinn, S.J. used by permission of Geoffrey Chapman, a division of Cassell Ltd.

Permission to reprint the *Gloria Patri, Gloria in Excelsis Deo, Te Deum, Benedictus, Magnificat* and *Nunc Dimittis.* International Consultation of English Texts. Prayers We Have in Common, © 1975.

Permission to reprint verses from Massey Shepherd's translation of Psalm 118, from *A Liturgical Psalter for the Christian Year,* copyright by The Order of St. Benedict, Inc. Published by The Liturgical Press, Collegeville, Minnesota. Used with permission.

Excerpt(s) from *The Jerusalem Bible,* copyright © 1966 by Darton, Longman & Todd, Ltd. and Doubleday & Company, Inc. are reprinted by permission of the Publisher.

Library of Congress
Catalog Card Number: 85-60409

ISBN: 0-8091-2718-0

Published by Paulist Press
997 Macarthur Boulevard
Mahwah, New Jersey 07430

Printed and bound in the
United States of America

INTRODUCTION

Like other men and women, Christians are constantly in danger of forgetting the central facts of their vocation. Recalling, remembering, memorializing—"until he comes again"—is of the essence of being a Christian. For the believer, Jesus is the central fact of human history, and his life, death, resurrection and coming again are the focus of Christian existence. To forget the facts of his saving career is to step into meaninglessness; to remember them prayfully is to enter into the very meaning of human life.

"Let us keep our eyes fixed on Jesus" is an exhortation that undergirds the essential structures of Church life, shapes and molds its liturgies, and produces the innumerable devotional practices that dot its history. Keeping the memory of Jesus fresh and green requires effort, imagination and genius—"Lest We Forget."

Like the Rosary of the Blessed Virgin Mary and the Way of the Cross—to name only two popular devotions—this set of devotions concentrates on a series of central mysteries in the life of our Lord. To highlight and concentrate on these thirty-one

1

mysteries, it selects two key readings from Holy Scripture for each day of the month and surrounds them with psalms, canticles and prayers in order to enhance each mystery-event and help us meditate on its meaning. Each of the thirty-one mysteries is designed to be a true liturgy of the Word for personal or group use.

The basic enemy of all sound religion is superficiality, shallowness, lack of commitment. The apparent believer lives on the surface of things, and ignores or skirts the Mystery of Christ. Such a person is content with the shell and forgets the kernel, takes the chaff and leaves the grain, settles for mere doctrines and neglects knowing Jesus in person.

On the other hand, the meditative believer discovers that all the events of Christ's life are "mysteries," that is, they are incidents which have a mystical significance concealed within their depths. Devotion, prayerful concentration, heartfelt attention bring to the surface their hidden depths and transform the believer in the process. The past even becomes a present, saving event in the here-and-now of daily existence; it warms and stirs the believer's heart and fixes the eyes of faith on Jesus "on whom our faith depends from beginning to end."

This set of biblical devotions invites the user "to read, mark, learn and inwardly digest" the Word of God, that is, Christ himself as he moves from the womb of the Virgin Mary—through his birth, public life, passion, death, resurrection—to his final coming again in glory to judge the living and the dead. Some devotions concentrate more on the passion and death of Jesus, some more on his birth and childhood. Like the classic Dominican Rosary in fifteen mysteries, these devotions focus on the whole Mystery of Christ—on his joys, on his sorrows, and on the blessed events in which he is and will be revealed as the Lord of Glory.

HOW TO MEDITATE

In down-to-earth Hebrew, to *meditate* is to chew one's cud. The familiar cattle of Hebrew existence provided a helpful image for the devout believer "whose delight is the law of the Lord and who ponders his law day and night" (Ps 1). The browsing cow nibbles constantly at the lush pasture and when she has filled her stomach lies down, regurgitates what she has gathered and chews "meditatively" on her cud until it is fully assimilated.

Those who want to ponder the Gospel can do likewise. They need to frequent the fresh green pastures of the Word of God, chew it over deliberately and carefully, and ruminate upon it until they are nourished, enriched and strengthened in the process.

More practically, meditation requires a certain amount of leisure, repose and silence. Haste,

noise and distraction are the death of devotion.
That means that busy people have to be ingenious
in finding the right time, place and posture for
meditating well. The Word of God can only
challenge and convert us if we *listen* to it.

Finally, it must always be remembered that inner
prayer is a free gift of the Holy Spirit. It can be
prepared by attention and devotion but it must
also be *awaited* in patience and docility. We have
to pray for the gift of prayer.

Open my mouth, O Lord, to praise your holy
    Name.
Cleanse my heart from all vain, evil or distracting
    thoughts.
Enlighten my understanding and warm my heart
that I may worthily recite this Office with attention
    and devotion,
and deserve to be heard in the presence of your
    divine Majesty.
Through Christ our Lord. Amen.

Roman Breviary

Your Word, O Lord, is a lamp for my feet,
    A light for my path.

Psalm 119:105

DIRECTIONS FOR GROUP USE
This prayer book is designed to be used both by
individuals and by groups.

Individuals normally read the selections for each day as they stand, pausing whenever they feel like meditating on what they have just read. The rule here is always quality before quantity.

Groups need a bit more formality in order to facilitate the participation of all who are present. It is usually convenient to have at least a Leader of group prayer and a Reader for the Scripture lessons.

An example:
The Leader recites the opening Call to Prayer:
> Come. Let us adore the Word made flesh, alleluia!

All respond:
> *Come, let us adore Christ, our Lord, alleluia!*

PSALM OR CANTICLE

The Leader recites the antiphon in full:
> Hosanna to the Son of David! Hosanna in the highest!

All repeat the antiphon:
> *Hosanna to the Son of David! Hosanna in the highest!*

Then the Leader reads the psalm, stanza by stanza, and all repeat the antiphon as a refrain between each stanza. All say the antiphon a final time after the recitation of the ''Glory to the Father.''

PSALM PRAYER

The Leader then says: Let us pray.

All pause for a few minutes of silent/personal
    prayer on the psalm.

The Leader then says the psalm prayer and all
    answer: *Amen.*

FIRST READING

The Reader announces the first lesson:
    A Reading from the Prophet Isaiah.
and reads the assigned passage with the care and
reverence befitting the Word of God.

RESPONSORY

The responsory is an interlude between the two
    readings.

The Leader says:

Holy, holy, holy! The Lord almighty is holy!

All repeat this refrain:

Holy, holy, holy! The Lord almighty is holy!

Leader:

His glory fills the whole world.

All:

Holy, holy, holy! The Lord almighty is holy!

Leader:

Glory to the Father, and to the Son, and to the
    Holy Spirit.

All:

Holy, holy, holy! The Lord almighty is holy!

SECOND READING

The Reader announces the second lesson:
> A Reading from the Good News according to St. Luke.

and reads the Gospel selection.

All pause for silent reflection on the two readings.

VERSICLE

To conclude the pause for silent reflection, the Leader recites the versicle:
> When Christ was about to come into the world, he said:

And All respond:
> *Here I am to do your will, O God.*

CANTICLE

The Leader and the group recite the canticle as they did the opening psalm.

FINAL PRAYER

At the conclusion of the canticle, the Leader again invites the group to silent prayer: Let us pray.
All answer *Amen* to the prayer.

BLESSING

The Leader recites the blessing.
All make the sign of the cross and say: *Amen*.

ALTERNATIVE METHOD OF PSALMODY

The Psalm or Canticle may be alternated between the Leader and the group, stanza by stanza, with

the antiphon being repeated only before and after
the text of the Psalm or Canticle, and once more
after the "Glory to the Father."

POSTURE
Postures at prayer will depend largely on whether
it is private or common prayer. In private, one
may, of course, take any posture that is conducive
to recollection and attention during prayer. Many
will want to adopt some of the suggestions made
for common prayer, such as standing and bowing
for the "Glory to the Father."

When a group of persons prays together, the
following suggestions may be of assistance.

Before the opening versicles (which serve as a call
to prayer), all may sit or kneel in silence for a few
moments and make a serious attempt at
recollecting themselves in the presence of God
who summons them to hear and heed the Gospel
of Christ.

Then all stand, turn to the east (whence Christ
shall return in glory to judge the living and the
dead) and alternate the opening versicles.

They may stand for the Psalm/Canticle, bow
profoundly for the "Glory to the Father, and to the

8

Son, and to the Holy Spirit," kneel for the pause for silent prayer, and stand for the psalm prayer.

Sitting is appropriate for the first lesson and its responsory and standing for the Gospel. One may also make the sign of the cross on forehead, lips and breast when the Gospel is announced.

Let us keep our eyes fixed on Jesus,
on whom our faith depends from beginning to
end,
He did not give up because of the cross!
On the contrary,
because of the joy that was waiting for Him,
He thought nothing of the disgrace of dying on the
cross,
and He is now seated at the right side of God's
throne.

Heb 12:2

DAY 1

The Angel Gabriel
Brings the Message to Mary

Into the desert of our lives descends the Word of life and light, the Gift of the Father, the work of the Spirit. Mary's "Yes" is our response to the loving initiative of God-in-Christ.

Come, let us adore the Word made flesh, alleluia!
Come, let us adore Christ our Lord, alleluia!

Canticle of Isaiah (35:10–10): God Comes to Save Us
Antiphon: Hosanna to the Son of David! Hosanna in the highest!

The desert will rejoice,
the flowers will bloom in the wastelands.
The desert will sing and shout for joy;
it will be as beautiful as the Lebanon Mountains
and as fertile as the fields of Carmel and Sharon.
Everyone will see the Lord's splendor,
see his greatness and power.

Give strength to hands that are tired
and to knees that tremble with weakness.
Tell everyone who is discouraged,

"Be strong and don't be afraid!
God is coming to your rescue."

The blind will be able to see,
and the deaf will hear.
The lame will leap and dance,
and those who cannot speak will shout for joy.
Streams of water will flow through the desert;
the burning sand will become like a lake,
and dry land will be filled with springs.

There will be a highway there,
called "The Road of Holiness."
No sinner will ever travel that road;
no fools will mislead those who follow it.
Those whom the Lord has rescued
will travel home by that road.
They will reach Jerusalem with gladness,
singing and shouting for joy.

Glory to the Father, and to the Son, and to the
     Holy Spirit:
as it was in the beginning, is now, and will be for
     ever. Amen.

Prayer
Loving Father,
you created human nature in all its nobility
and still more marvelously renewed it.
Grant that through this wondrous mystery
we may have fellowship in the Godhead of Jesus
     Christ

who humbled himself to share our humanity;
he lives and reigns with you and the Holy Spirit,
one God, now and for ever.
Amen.

A Reading from the Prophet Isaiah (7:14–16)

The Lord himself will give you a sign: a young woman who is pregnant will have a son and will name him "Immanuel": God-is-with-us. By the time he is old enough to make his own decisions, people will be drinking milk and eating honey.

Responsory

Holy, holy, holy! The Lord almighty is holy!
Holy, holy, holy! The Lord almighty is holy!
His glory fills the whole world.
Holy, holy, holy! The Lord almighty is holy!
Glory to the Father, and to the Son, and to the
    Holy Spirit.
Holy, holy, holy! The Lord almighty is holy!

A Reading from the Good News according to St. Luke (1:26–38)

God sent the angel Gabriel to a town in Galilee named Nazareth. He had a message for a girl promised in marriage to a man named Joseph, who was a descendant of King David. The girl's name was Mary. The angel came to her and said, "Peace be with you! The Lord is with you and has greatly blessed you! You will give birth to a son, and you will name him Jesus. He will be great and will be called the Son of the Most High God. The

Lord God will make him a king, as his ancestor
David was, and he will be king of the descendants
of Jacob for ever; his kingdom will never end." "I
am the Lord's servant," said Mary; "may it
happen to me as you have said." And the angel
left her.

When Christ was about to come into the world,
    he said:
Here I am to do your will, O God.

Canticle of Mary (Luke 1:46–55)
*Antiphon: You will give birth to a son and name
    him Jesus.*

My soul proclaims the greatness of the Lord,
my spirit rejoices in God my Savior;
for he has looked with favor on his lowly servant.

From this day all generations will call me blessed:
the Almighty has done great things for me,
and holy is his Name.

He has mercy on those who fear him
in every generation.
He has shown the strength of his arm,
he has scattered the proud in their conceit.

He has cast down the mighty from their thrones,
and has lifted up the lowly.
He has filled the hungry with good things,
and the rich he has sent away empty.

He has come to the help of his servant Israel
for he has remembered his promise of mercy,
the promise he made to our ancestors,
to Abraham and Sarah and their children for ever.

Glory to the Father, and to the Son and to the
    Holy Spirit:
as it was in the beginning, is now, and will be for
    ever. Amen.

Prayer
Lord,
fill our hearts with your grace:
once, through the message of an angel
you revealed to us the incarnation of your Son;
now, through his suffering and death
lead us to the glory of his resurrection.
We ask this through Christ our Lord.
Amen.

Blessing
May the Word made flesh, full of grace and truth,
† bless us and keep us.
Amen.

DAY 2

Mary Visits Her Cousin Elizabeth

Impelled by the Spirit, Mary, the God-bearing-Virgin, hurries across the hills of Judea to bring the Good News to her relatives, Zachary and Elizabeth. She is the first bearer of the Good News, the first missionary, the first apostle.

Come, let us celebrate the visit of Mary and Elizabeth, alleluia.
Come, let us adore Christ, the Son of Mary, alleluia.

Canticle of Judith (13:18–20, 15:9): Mary, God's Valiant Daughter

Antiphon: Blessed are you among women and blessed is the fruit of your womb!

Blessed are you, daughter, by the Most High God, above all women on earth.
And blessed be the Lord God,
the creator of heaven and earth,
who guided your blow
at the head of the chief of our enemies.

Your deed of hope will never be forgotten
by those who tell of the might of God.
May God make this redound to your everlasting
    honor,
rewarding you with blessings
because you risked your life
when your people were being oppressed,
and you averted our disaster,
walking uprightly before our God.

You are the glory of Jerusalem,
the surpassing joy of Israel,
the splendid boast of our people.

Glory to the Father, and to the Son, and to the
    Holy Spirit:
as it was in the beginning, is now, and will be for
    ever. Amen.

Prayer
Gracious God,
the childbearing of the blessed Virgin
was the beginning of our salvation:
may this festival of her visitation
bring us an increase of peace.
Through Christ our Lord.
Amen.

A Reading from Paul the Apostle to the Galatians (4:4–6)
When the right time finally came, God sent his
own Son. He came as the son of a human mother

and lived under the Jewish Law, to redeem those who were under the Law, so that they might become God's children. To show that you are his children, God sent the Spirit of his Son into our hearts, the Spirit who cries out, "Father, my Father."

Responsory

From this day all generations will call me blessed.
From this day all generations will call me blessed.
The Almighty has done great things for me.
From this day all generations will call me blessed.
Glory to the Father, and to the Son, and to the
     Holy Spirit.
From this day all generations will call me blessed.

A Reading from the Good News according to St. Luke (1:39–42)

Mary got ready and hurried off to a town in the hill country of Judea. She went into Zechariah's house and greeted Elizabeth. When Elizabeth heard Mary's greeting, the baby moved within her. Elizabeth was filled with the Holy Spirit and said in a loud voice, "You are the most blessed of all women, and blessed is the child you will bear."

Blessed are they who hear the word of God.
And keep it.

Canticle of Zachary (Luke 1:68–79)

*Antiphon: Blessed is the womb that bore you, O
          Christ, and the breasts that nursed you.*

Blessed be the Lord, the God of Israel;
he has come to his people and set them free.

He has raised up for us a mighty savior,
born of the house of his servant David.

Through his holy prophets he promised of old
that he would save us from our enemies,
from the hands of all who hate us.

He promised to show mercy to our ancestors
and to remember his holy covenant.

This was the oath he swore to our father Abraham:
to set us free from the hands of our enemies,
free to worship him without fear,
holy and righteous in his sight
all the days of our life.

You, my child, shall be called the prophet of the
     Most High,
for you will go before the Lord to prepare his way,
to give his people knowledge of salvation
by the forgiveness of their sins.

In the tender compassion of our God
the dawn from on high shall break upon us,
to shine on those who dwell in darkness and the
     shadow of death,
and to guide our feet into the way of peace.

Glory to the Father, and to the Son, and to the
    Holy Spirit:
as it was in the beginning, is now, and will be for
    ever. Amen.

Prayer
Eternal Father,
you inspired the Virgin Mary, mother of your Son,
to visit Elizabeth and assist her in her need.
Keep us open to the working of your Spirit,
and with Mary may we praise you forever.
We ask this through Christ our Lord.
Amen.

Blessing
May Christ, the sun of righteousness,
† bless us and keep us.
Amen.

DAY 3

The Birth of Jesus

The darkness of this world is illumined by heavenly messengers, heavenly light and celestial music announcing Good News/Great Joy to the poor and lowly. They/we praise God "for all we have heard and seen."

A Child is born for us, alleluia!
Come, let us adore him, alleluia!

Hymn
A noble flow'r of Juda from tender roots has
    sprung,
A rose from stem of Jesse, as prophets long had
    sung,
A blossom fair and bright,
That in the midst of winter will change to dawn
    our night.

The rose of grace and beauty of which Isaiah sings
Is Mary, virgin mother, and Christ the flower she
    brings.
By God's divine decree
She bore our loving Savior, who died to set us
    free.

To Mary, dearest mother, with fervent hearts we
  pray:
Grant that your tender infant will cast our sins
  away,
And guide us with his love
That we shall ever serve him, and live with him
  above.

Psalm 2: God's Chosen Son, our Messianic King

Antiphon: Glory to God in the highest and peace
    to his people on earth.

Why do the nations plan rebellion?
Why do people make their useless plots?
Their kings revolt,
their rulers plot together against the Lord
and against the king he chose.
"Let us free ourselves from their rule," they say;
"let us throw off their control."

From his throne in heaven the Lord laughs
and mocks their feeble plans.
Then he warns them in anger
and terrifies them with his fury.
"Oh Zion, my sacred hill," he says,
"I have installed my king."

"I will announce," says the king,
"what the Lord has declared.
He said to me: 'You are my son;
today I have become your father.
Ask, and I will give you all the nations;

the whole earth will be yours.
You will break them with an iron rod;
you will shatter them in pieces like a clay pot.' ''

Now listen to this warning, you kings;
learn this lesson, you rulers of the world:
Serve the Lord with fear;
tremble and bow down to him;
or else his anger will be quickly aroused,
and you will suddenly die.

Glory to the Father, and to the Son, and to the
    Holy Spirit:
as it was in the beginning, is now, and will be for
    ever. Amen.

Prayer
God of power and might,
the glory of all who believe in you,
fill the world with your splendor
and show the nations the light of your truth.
We ask this through Christ our Lord.
Amen.

A Reading from Paul the Apostle
to the Romans (1:2–4)
The Good News was promised long ago by God
through his prophets, as written in the Holy
Scriptures. It is about his Son, our Lord Jesus
Christ: as to his humanity, he was born a
descendant of David; as to his divine holiness, he

was shown with great power to be the Son of God
by being raised from death.

Responsory
The Word was made flesh, alleluia, alleluia!
The Word was made flesh, alleluia, alleluia!
And dwelt among us, alleluia, alleluia!
The Word was made flesh, alleluia, alleluia!
Glory to the Father, and to the Son, and to the
     Holy Spirit.
The Word was made flesh, alleluia, alleluia!

A Reading from the Good News according
to St. Luke (2:9–11)
An angel of the Lord appeared to the shepherds
and the glory of the Lord shone over them. They
were terribly afraid, but the angel said to them,
"Don't be afraid! I am here with good news for
you, which will bring great joy to all the people.
This very day in David's town your Savior was
born—Christ the Lord!"

The shepherds went back singing praises to God.
For all they had heard and seen.

The Great Doxology
Glory to God in the highest,
     and peace to his people on earth.

Lord God, heavenly King,
almighty God and Father,

we worship you, we give you thanks,
we praise you for your glory.

Lord Jesus Christ, only Son of the Father,
Lord God, Lamb of God,
you take away the sin of the world:
   have mercy on us;

you are seated at the right hand of the Father:
   receive our prayer.

For you alone are the Holy One,
you alone are the Lord,
you alone are the Most High,
   Jesus Christ,
   with the Holy Spirit,
   in the glory of God the Father. Amen.

Prayer
Lord God,
we praise you for creating the human race
and still more for restoring it in Christ.
Your Son shared our weakness;
may we share his glory,
for he lives and reigns with you and the Holy
     Spirit,
one God, for ever and ever.
Amen.

Blessing
May the Son of God become the Son of Man
† bless us and keep us.
Amen.

DAY 4

The Visit of the Magi

Those who studied the stars and followed the heavenly signs become the first-fruits of those who believe. The Magi and the Shepherds "shout together with joy" as "the glory of the Lord" dawns upon them.

The Lord has shown forth his glory.
Come, let us adore him.

Psalm 72: Jesus is the King of Justice and Peace
Antiphon: Seeing the Child with Mary his mother, the Magi knelt in worship.

Teach the king to judge with your righteousness,
    O God;
share with him your own justice,
so that he will rule over your people with justice
and govern the oppressed with righteousness.
May your people worship you as long as the sun
    shines,
as long as the moon gives light,
for ages to come.

May the king be like rain on the fields,
like showers falling on the land.
May righteousness flourish in his lifetime,
and may prosperity last as long as the moon gives
     light.

His kingdom will reach from sea to sea,
from the Euphrates to the ends of the earth.
The peoples of the desert will bow down before
     him;
his enemies will throw themselves to the ground.
The kings of Spain and of the islands will offer him
     gifts;
the kings of Arabia and Ethiopia will bring him
     offerings.
All kings will bow down before him;
all nations will serve him.

He rescues the poor who call to him,
and those who are needy and neglected.
He has pity on the weak and poor;
he saves the lives of those in need.
He rescues them from oppression and violence;
their lives are precious to him.
Long live the king!
May he be given gold from Arabia;
may prayers be said for him at all times;
may God's blessing be on him always!

May the king's name never be forgotten;
may his fame last as long as the sun.
May all nations praise him,

may they ask God to bless them
and may they wish happiness for the king.

Glory to the Father, and to the Son, and to the
    Holy Spirit:
as it was in the beginning, is now, and will be for
    ever. Amen.

Prayer
Almighty God,
you gave the kingdom of justice and peace
to David and to his descendant,
our Lord Jesus Christ.
Extend this kingdom to the whole family of
    nations,
give peace to all peoples,
justice to the poor
and relief to the destitute,
in the name of the same Christ our Lord.
Amen.

A Reading from the Prophet Isaiah (52:7–8)
How wonderful it is to see a messenger coming
across the mountains, bringing good news, the
news of peace! He announces victory and says to
Zion, "Your God is king!" Those who guard the
city are shouting, shouting together for joy. They
can see with their own eyes the return of the Lord
to Zion.

Responsory

All kings will bow down before him.
All kings will bow down before him.
All nations will serve him.
All kings will bow down before him.
Glory to the Father, and to the Son, and to the
    Holy Spirit.
All kings will bow down before him.

A Reading from the Good News according to St. Matthew (2:1–2, 9–11)

Jesus was born in the town of Bethlehem in Judea, during the time when Herod was king. Soon afterward, some men who studied the stars came from the East to Jerusalem and asked, "Where is the baby born to be the king of the Jews? We saw his star when it came up in the East, and we have come to worship him." . . . And on their way to Bethlehem they saw the same star they had seen in the East. When they saw it, how happy they were, what joy was theirs! It went ahead of them until it stopped over the place where the child was. They went into the house, and when they saw the child with his mother, Mary, they knelt down and worshipped him. They brought out their gifts of gold, frankincense, and myrrh, and presented them to him.

I will send my messenger.
To prepare the way before me.

Canticle of Isaiah (60:1–3, 11a, 14c, 18–19)

*Antiphon: The Magi offered royal gold to
acknowledge a great King,
sweet frankincense to adore a true
God,
dusty myrrh to confess his coming
death.*

Arise, shine for your light has come,
and the glory of the Lord has dawned upon you.
For behold, darkness covers the land;
deep gloom enshrouds the peoples.
But over you the Lord will rise,
and his glory will appear upon you.
Nations will stream to your light,
and kings to the brightness of your dawning.

Your gates will always be open;
by day or night they will never be shut.
They will call you, The City of the Lord,
The Zion of the Holy One of Israel.
Violence will no more be heard in your land,
ruin or destruction within your borders.
You will call your walls, Salvation,
and all your portals, Praise.

The sun will no more be your light by day;
by night you will not need the brightness of the
moon.
The Lord will be your glory.

Glory to the Father, and to the Son, and to the
    Holy Spirit:
as it was in the beginning, is now, and will be for
    ever. Amen.

Prayer

Father, you revealed your Son to the nations
by the guidance of a star.
Lead us to the glory of heaven
by the light of faith.
Through the same Christ our Lord.
Amen.

Blessing

May Jesus Christ, the light of the world,
† bless us and keep us.
Amen.

DAY 5

Jesus Is Presented in the Temple

As Mary and Joseph present their first-born to YHWH, another God-fearing couple, Simeon and Anna, welcome the Lord of the Temple, the Light of the nations and the Glory of Israel.

Come, let us worship the Lord of creation.
He enters his holy temple.

Psalm 48: God Comes To Claim His Own
Antiphon: The parents of Jesus brought him to Jerusalem to present him to the Lord.

Zion, the mountain of God, is high and beautiful;
the city of the great king brings joy to all the
world.
God has shown that there is safety with him
inside the fortresses of the city.

The kings gathered together
and came to attack Mount Zion.
But when they saw it, they were amazed;
they were afraid and ran away.
There they were seized with fear and anguish,

like a woman about to bear a child,
like ships tossing in a furious storm.

We have heard what God has done,
and now we have seen it
in the city of our God, the Lord Almighty;
he will keep the city safe forever.

Inside your Temple, O God,
we think of your constant love.
You are praised by people everywhere,
and your fame extends over all the earth.
You rule with justice;
let the people of Zion be glad!
You give right judgments;
let there be joy in the cities of Judah!

Glory to the Father, and to the Son, and to the
    Holy Spirit:
as it was in the beginning, is now, and will be for
    ever. Amen.

Prayer
Lord Jesus Christ,
you appeared among us
in the likeness of our flesh,
and were presented in the Temple
by your parents according to the Law.
Enlightened by the Holy Spirit,
the old man Simeon recognized, welcomed and
    blessed you.

Grant that we, too, enlightened and taught by the
    Holy Spirit,
may truly know you and faithfully love you,
now in this present life and through all the ages of
    ages.
Amen.

A Reading from the Prophet Malachi (3:1)

The Lord Almighty answers, "I will send my
messenger to prepare the way for me. Then the
Lord you are looking for will suddenly come to his
Temple. The messenger you long to see will come
and proclaim my convenant."

Responsory

Old Simeon took the child Jesus in his arms.
Old Simeon took the child Jesus in his arms.
And the child was the old man's guide.
Old Simeon took the child Jesus in his arms.
Glory to the Father, and to the Son, and to the
    Holy Spirit.
Old Simeon took the child Jesus in his arms.

A Reading from the Good News according to St. Luke (2:22, 25–28)

The time came for Joseph and Mary to perform the
ceremony of purification, as the Law of Moses
commanded. So they took the child to Jerusalem
to present him to the Lord. At that time there was
a man named Simeon living in Jerusalem. He was
a good, God-fearing man and was waiting for
Israel to be saved. The Holy Spirit was with him

and had assured him that he would not die before
he had seen the Lord's promised Messiah. Led by
the Spirit, Simeon went into the Temple. When
his parents brought the child Jesus into the Temple
to do for him what the Law required, Simeon took
the child in his arms and gave thanks to God:

The Canticle of Simeon (Luke 2:29–32)
Antiphon: A light to reveal you to the nations,
and the glory of your people Israel.

Lord, now you let your servant go in peace;
your word has been fulfilled:

my own eyes have seen the salvation
which you have prepared in the sight of every
     people:

a light to reveal you to the nations
and the glory of your people Israel.

Glory to the Father, and to the Son, and to the
     Holy Spirit:
as it was in the beginning, is now, and will be for
     ever. Amen.

Prayer
All-powerful Father,
Christ your Son became human for us
and was presented in the temple.

May he free our hearts from sin
and bring us into your presence.
We ask this through Christ our Lord.
Amen.

Blessing
May Christ, Son of Mary and Son of God,
† bless us and keep us.
Amen.

DAY 6

Jesus Is Baptized by John in the Jordan

At the waters of the Jordan, God opens the heavens, blesses the air, cleanses the waters, and through the Holy Spirit shows us his only Son. "The Kingdom of God is at hand!"

Christ has appeared to us.
Come, let us adore him.

Psalm 89: Jesus Inherits the Promise Made to David

Antiphon: You are my own dear Son. I am pleased with you.

In a vision long ago you said to your faithful
  servants,
"I have given help to a famous soldier;
I have given the throne to one I chose from the
  people.
I have made my servant David king
by anointing him with holy oil.
My strength will always be with him,
my power will make him strong.
His enemies will never succeed against him;
the wicked will not defeat him.

I will crush his foes
and kill everyone who hates him.
I will love him and be loyal to him;
I will make him always victorious.

He will say of me,
'You are my father and my God;
you are my protector and savior.'
I will make him my first-born son,
the greatest of all kings.
I will always keep my promise to him,
and my covenant with him will last forever.
His dynasty will be as permanent as the sky;
a descendant of his will always be king.''

Glory to the Father, and to the Son, and to the
    Holy Spirit:
as it was in the beginning, is now, and will be for
    ever. Amen.

Prayer
Almighty, eternal God,
when the Spirit descended upon Jesus
at his baptism in the Jordan,
you revealed him as your own beloved Son.
Keep us, your children, born of water and the
    Spirit,
faithful to our calling.
We ask this through Christ our Lord.
Amen.

A Reading from the Prophet Isaiah (61:1–2)

The Sovereign Lord has filled me with his spirit. He has chosen me and sent me to bring good news to the poor, to heal the broken-hearted, to announce release to captives, and freedom to those in prison. He has sent me to proclaim that the time has come when the Lord will save his people and defeat his enemies.

Responsory

Turn away from your sins and be baptized.
Turn away from your sins and be baptized.
The Kingdom of God is at hand.
Turn away from your sins and be baptized.
Glory to the Father, and to the Son, and to the
    Holy Spirit.
Turn away from your sins and be baptized.

A Reading from the Good News according to St. Mark (1:9–13)

Jesus came from Nazareth in the province of Galilee, and was baptized by John in the Jordan. As soon as Jesus came up out of the water, he saw heaven opening and the Spirit coming down on him like a dove. And a voice came from heaven, ''You are my own dear Son. I am pleased with you.'' And at once the Spirit made him go into the desert, where he stayed forty days, being tempted by Satan. Wild animals were there also, but angels came and helped him.

I baptize you with water, said John.
But he will baptize you with the Holy Spirit.

Canticle of Isaiah (42:1-8)
Antiphon: I will make him my first-born Son.

Here is my servant, whom I strengthen—
the one I have chosen,
with whom I am pleased.
I have filled him with my spirit,
and he will bring justice to every nation.

He will not shout or raise his voice
or make loud speeches in the streets.
He will not break off a bent reed
nor put out a flickering lamp.
He will bring lasting justice to all.
He will not lose hope or courage;
he will establish justice on the earth.
Distant lands eagerly wait for his teaching.

Glory to the Father, and to the Son, and to the
    Holy Spirit:
as it was in the beginning, is now, and will be for
    ever. Amen.

Prayer
Lord Jesus Christ,
you humbled yourself,
received baptism at the hands of your forerunner,
and were proclaimed God's own dear Son.
Grant that we who have been baptized into you
may rejoice in our divine adoption
and show ourselves the servants of all;
for yours is the power and the glory,

now and for ever.
Amen.

Blessing
May Christ Jesus, God's own dear Son,
† bless us and keep us.
Amen.

DAY 7

Jesus Begins His Work in Galilee

The obscurity and silence of the hidden life at Nazareth come to a close; the Light shines forth, the Word speaks: "Repent, believe, be baptized!" Those who walk in the darkness shall see a great light.

Come, let us adore Christ, our King and our God.
And bow down before him.

Psalm 96: The Messianic Kingdom
Antiphon: Worship the Lord in the beauty of holiness!

Sing a new song to the Lord!
Sing to the Lord, all the world!
Sing to the Lord, and praise him!
Proclaim every day the good news
that he has saved us.
Proclaim his glory to the nations,
his mighty acts to all peoples.

The Lord is great and is to be highly praised;
he is to be honored more than all the gods.
The gods of all other nations are only idols,
but the Lord created the heavens.
Glory and majesty surround him;
power and beauty fill his Temple.

Praise the Lord, all people on earth;
praise his glory and might.
Praise the Lord's glorious name;
bring an offering and come into his Temple.
Bow down before the Holy One when he appears;
tremble before him, all the earth!

Say to all the nations, ''The Lord is King!''
The earth is set firmly in place
and cannot be moved;
he will judge the people with justice.''
Be glad, earth and sky!

Roar, sea, and every creature in you;
be glad, fields, and everything in you!
The trees in the wood will shout for joy
when the Lord comes to rule the earth.
He will rule the peoples of the world
with justice and fairness.

Glory to the Father, and to the Son, and to the
    Holy Spirit:
as it was in the beginning, is now, and will be for
    ever. Amen.

Prayer
God of glory and majesty,
ruler of all the powers-that-be,
as we worship before you in the beauty of
    holiness,
bring to completion the promised kingdom
of justice, peace and love,
through Jesus Christ our Lord.
Amen.

A Reading from the Acts of the Apostles (10:36–38)
You know the message he sent to the people of
Israel, proclaiming the Good News of peace
through Jesus Christ, who is Lord of all. You know
of the great event that took place throughout the
land of Israel, beginning in Galilee after John
preached his message of baptism. You know
about Jesus of Nazareth and how God poured out
on him the Holy Spirit and power. He went
everywhere, doing good and healing all who were
under the power of the Devil, for God was with
him.

Responsory
The people who walk in darkness shall see a great
    light.
*The people who walk in darkness shall see a great
    light.*
The dawn from on high shall break upon them.
*The people who walk in darkness shall see a great
    light.*

Glory to the Father, and to the Son, and to the
Holy Spirit.
*The people who walk in darkness shall see a great
light.*

A Reading from the Good News according
to St. Matthew (4:12–13, 17, 23, 25)

When Jesus heard that John had been put in
prison, he went away to Galilee. He did not stay
in Nazareth, but went to live in Capernaum, a
town by Lake Galilee. From that time Jesus began
to preach his message: "Turn away from your
sins, because the Kingdom of heaven is near!"
Jesus went all over Galilee, teaching in the
synagogues, preaching the Good News about the
Kingdom, and healing people who had all kinds
of disease and sickness. Large crowds followed
him from Galilee and the Ten Towns, from
Jerusalem, Judea, and the land on the other side of
the Jordan.

On those who live in the dark land of death.
Light will shine.

Canticle of Isaiah (55:6–11)
Antiphon: Repent and believe the Gospel.

Seek the Lord while he wills to be found;
call upon him when he draws near.
Let the wicked forsake their ways

and the evil ones their thoughts;
And let them turn to the Lord, and he will have
   compassion,
and to our God, for he will richly pardon.
For my thoughts are not your thoughts,
nor your ways my ways, says the Lord.
For as the heavens are higher than the earth,
so are my ways higher than your ways,
and my thoughts than your thoughts.

For as rain and snow fall from the heavens
and return not again, but water the earth,
bringing forth life and giving growth,
seed for sowing and bread for eating,
so is my word that goes forth from my mouth;
it will not return to me empty;
but it will accomplish that which I have purposed,
and prosper in that for which I sent it.

Glory to the Father, and to the Son, and to the
   Holy Spirit:
as it was in the beginning, is now, and will be for
   ever. Amen.

Prayer
Give us grace, O Lord,
to answer readily the call of our Savior Jesus Christ
and proclaim to all people the Good News of his
   salvation,

that we and the whole world may perceive
the glory of his marvelous works;
who lives and reigns with you and the Holy Spirit,
one God, for ever and ever.
Amen.

Blessing
May the Lord of all, the proclaimer of the Good
    News of peace,
† bless us and keep us.
Amen.

DAY 8

The Sermon on the Mount

A new and greater Moses goes up the mountainside; a new, fresh, fuller revelation blesses the ears of humankind. Now the Preacher is the Son of God himself and the Message is "sweeter than the purest honey and finer than the finest gold." Happy are they who hunger and thirst for the teaching of Jesus.

Come, let us worship the teacher of righteousness.
And bow down before him.

Psalm 19B: The Law of the Lord
Antiphon: Your will be done!

The law of the Lord is perfect;
it gives new strength.
The commands of the Lord are trustworthy,
giving wisdom to those who lack it.
The laws of the Lord are right,
and those who obey them are happy.
The commands of the Lord are just
and give understanding to the mind.
The worship of the Lord is good;
it will continue for ever.

The judgments of the Lord are just;
they are always fair.
They are more desirable than the finest gold;
they are sweeter than the purest honey.
They give knowledge to me, your servant;
I am rewarded for obeying them.

No one can see his own errors;
deliver me, Lord, from hidden faults!
Keep me safe, also, from willful sins;
don't let them rule over me.
Then I shall be perfect
and free from the evil of sin.

May my words and my thoughts be acceptable to
    you,
O Lord, my refuge and my redeemer!

Glory to the Father, and to the Son, and to the
    Holy Spirit:
as it was in the beginning, is now, and will be for
    ever. Amen.

Prayer
Holy God, our teacher and our lawgiver,
may your perfect law of love,
sweeter than honey and finer than gold,
be a light to our feet and a lamp to our path,
so that we may worship you truly
in union with all your saints,
now and for ever.
Amen.

A Reading from the Prophet Micah (6:1–8)
What shall I bring to the Lord, the God of heaven,
when I come to worship him? Shall I bring the
best calves to burn as offerings to him? Will the
Lord be pleased if I bring him thousands of sheep
or endless streams of olive oil? Shall I offer him
my first-born child to pay for my sins? No, the
Lord has told us what is good. What he requires of
us is this: to do what is just, to show constant
love, and to live in humble fellowship with our
God.

Responsory
May my words and my thoughts be acceptable to
    you.
*May my words and my thoughts be acceptable to
    you.*
O Lord, my refuge and my redeemer.
*May my words and my thoughts be acceptable to
    you.*
Glory to the Father, and to the Son, and to the
    Holy Spirit.
*May my words and my thoughts be acceptable to
    you.*

**A Reading from the Good News according to St.
Matthew (5:1–10)**
Seeing the crowds, Jesus went up the hill [near
Capernaum]. There he sat down and was joined
by his disciples. Then he began to speak. This is
what he taught them:

How happy are the poor in spirit;
theirs is the kingdom of heaven.
Happy the gentle;
they shall have the earth for their heritage.
Happy those who mourn;
they shall be comforted.
Happy those who hunger and thirst for what is
    right;
they shall be satisfied.
Happy the merciful;
they shall have mercy shown them.
Happy the pure in heart;
they shall see God.
Happy the peacemakers;
they shall be called children of God.
Happy those who are persecuted in the cause of
    right;
theirs is the kingdom of heaven.

You are the salt of the earth.
You are the light of the world.

Canticle of Isaiah (2:2–4)
*Antiphon: The crowd was amazed at the teaching
              of Jesus.*

In the days to come
the mountain where the Temple stands
will be the highest one of all,
towering above all the hills.

Many nations will come streaming to it,
and their people will say,
"Let us go up the hill of the Lord,
to the Temple of Israel's God.
He will teach us what he wants us to do;
we will walk in the paths he has chosen.
For the Lord's teaching comes from Jerusalem;
from Zion he speaks to his people."

He will settle disputes among great nations.
They will hammer their swords into plows
and their spears into pruning knives.
Nations will never again go to war,
never prepare for battle again.

Glory to the Father, and to the Son, and to the
    Holy Spirit:
as it was in the beginning, is now, and will be for
    ever. Amen.

Prayer
Almighty God,
our hope and our strength,
without you we falter.
Help us to follow Christ
and to live according to your will.
We ask this through Christ our Lord.
Amen.

Blessing
May Christ Jesus, the teacher of holiness,
† bless us and keep us.
Amen.

DAY 9

Signs of the Coming Kingdom

The Kingdom of God appears in power. As the designated Son and Heir, Jesus heals the sick, expels demons and offers hope to all. He is mighty in word and in deed.

Come, let us worship the Lord.
Our mighty God and Savior.

Psalm 147: Praise God Who Heals and Saves
Antiphon: God has raised up for us a mighty Savior.

It is good to sing praise to our God;
it is pleasant and right to praise him.
The Lord is restoring Jerusalem;
he is bringing back the exiles.
He heals the broken-hearted
and bandages their wounds.

He has decided the number of the stars
and calls each one by name.
Great and mighty is our Lord;

his wisdom cannot be measured.
He raises the humble,
but crushes the wicked to the ground.

Sing hymns of praise to the Lord;
play music on the harp to our God.
He spreads clouds over the sky;
he provides rain for the earth
and makes grass grow on the hills.
He gives animals their food
and feeds the young ravens when they call.

His pleasure is not in strong horses,
nor his delight in brave soldiers;
but he takes pleasure in those who honor him,
in those who trust in his constant love.

Glory to the Father, and to the Son, and to the
     Holy Spirit:
as it was in the beginning, is now, and will be for
     ever. Amen.

Prayer
Gracious God,
proclaimed by Jesus as our loving Father,
heal the broken-hearted
and bandage up the wounds of the human race,
that we may always find fresh reasons
for trusting in your constant love for us;
through Christ our Lord.
Amen.

A Reading from the Letter of Paul the Apostle to the Colossians (1:5–6, 12–13)

When the true message, the Good News, first came to you, you heard about the hope it offers. So your faith and love are based on what you hope for, which is kept safe for you in heaven. The gospel keeps bringing blessings and is spreading throughout the world. . . . With joy give thanks to the Father, who has made you fit to have your share of what God has reserved for his people in the kingdom of light. He rescued us from the power of darkness and brought us safe into the kingdom of his dear Son, by whom we are set free, that is, our sins are forgiven.

Responsory

Blessed is he who comes in the name of the Lord!
Blessed is he who comes in the name of the Lord!
Hosanna in the highest!
Blessed is he who comes in the name of the Lord!
Glory to the Father, and to the Son, and to the
    Holy Spirit.
Blessed is he who comes in the name of the Lord!

A Reading from the Good News according to St. Mark (1:32–34)

After the sun had set, and evening had come, people brought to Jesus all the sick and those who had demons. All the people of the town gathered in front of the house. Jesus healed many who were sick with all kinds of diseases and drove out many

demons. He would not let the demons say
anything, because they knew who he was.

He has done all things well!
He even makes the deaf hear and the dumb speak.

Canticle of Daniel (7:9–10, 13–14) Your Kingdom Come!
Antiphon: And he shall reign for ever and ever.

Thrones were set in place
and one of great age took his seat.
His robe was white as snow,
the hair of his head as pure as wool.
His throne was a blaze of flames,
its wheels were a burning fire.
A stream of fire poured out,
issuing from his presence.
A thousand thousand waited on him,
ten thousand times ten thousand stood before
    him.
A court was held
and the books were opened.

I gazed into the vision of the night.
And I saw, coming on the clouds of heaven,
one like a son of man.
He came to the one of great age
and was led into his presence.
On him was conferred sovereignty,
glory and kingship,
and all peoples, nations and languages became
    his servants.

His sovereignty is an eternal sovereignty
which shall never pass away,
nor will his empire ever be destroyed.

Glory to the Father, and to the Son, and to the
    Holy Spirit:
as it was in the beginning, is now, and will be for
    ever. Amen.

Prayer
Almighty and everlasting God,
you destroy the power of evil
and make all things new
in your dear Son Jesus Christ,
the King of kings and the Lord of lords;
heal the divisions of nations and peoples,
enslaved and divided by sin,
and subject us to the gracious rule of him
who lives and reigns with you and the Holy Spirit,
one God, now and for ever.
Amen.

Blessing
May Christ Jesus, the King of kings and the Lord of
lords, whose reign will never end,
† bless us and keep us.
Amen.

DAY 10

Jesus Chooses His Twelve Apostles

Jesus is the prime Apostle and Preacher of the Good News but he commissions and empowers a symbolic group of twelve apostles (heralds, envoys, messengers, missionaries) to be eye-witnesses to his resurrection, to preach the Good News to the very ends of the earth, to be the foundation-stones of the Universal Church, and, finally, to be martyrs, witnesses in blood, to the truth of the Gospel.

The Lord is the Apostle of the apostles.
Come, let us adore him.

Psalm 19A: Messengers of the Good News
Antiphon: The voice of the holy apostles is heard to the ends of the earth.

How clearly the sky reveals God's glory!
How plainly it shows what he has done!
Each day announces it to the following day;
each night repeats it to the next.
No speech or words are used,
no sound is heard;

yet their voice goes out to all the world
and is heard to the ends of the earth.

God made a home in the sky for the sun;
it comes out in the morning like a happy
    bridegroom,
like an athlete eager to run a race.
It starts at one end of the sky
and goes across to the other.
Nothing can hide from its heat.

Glory to the Father, and to the Son, and to the
    Holy Spirit:
as it was in the beginning, is now, and will be for
    ever. Amen.

Prayer
Almighty and everlasting God,
we thank you for your holy apostles
whom you called to preach the Gospel
to the whole world.
Raise up in this and every land
evangelists and heralds of your kingdom
that your Church may proclaim the unsearchable
    riches of our Savior Jesus Christ;
who lives and reigns with you and the Holy Spirit,
one God, now and for ever.
Amen.

A Reading from the Acts of the Apostles (5:39–42)

The Council called the apostles in, had them
whipped, and ordered them never again to speak

in the name of Jesus; and then they set them free. As the apostles left the Council, they were happy, because God had considered them worthy to suffer disgrace for the sake of Jesus. And every day in the Temple and in people's homes they continued to teach and preach the Good News about Jesus the Messiah.

Responsory

For my sake you will be brought to trial before
    rulers and kings.
For my sake you will be brought to trial before
    rulers and kings.
To tell the Good News to them.
For my sake you will be brought to trial before
    rulers and kings.
Glory to the Father, and to the Son, and to the
    Holy Spirit.
For my sake you will be brought to trial before
    rulers and kings.

A Reading from the Good News according to St. Mark (3:13–19)

Jesus went up a hill and called to himself the men he wanted. They came to him, and he chose twelve, whom he named apostles. "I have chosen you to be with me," he told them. "I will also send you out to preach, and you will have authority to drive out demons." These are the twelve he chose: Simon (Jesus gave him the name Peter); James and his brother John, the sons of Zebedee (Jesus gave them the name Boanerges, which means "Men of Thunder"); Andrew, Philip, Bartholomew, Matthew, Thomas, James son of Alpheus, Thaddeus, Simon the Patriot, and Judas Iscariot, who betrayed Jesus.

Go to all peoples everywhere and make them my
    disciples.
*Baptize them in the name of the Father, the Son
    and the Holy Spirit.*

Canticle of Isaiah (49:1–3, 6)
*Antiphon: With great power the apostles bore
        witness to the resurrection of the Lord
        Jesus.*

Listen to me, distant nations,
you people you live far away!

Before I was born, the Lord chose me
and appointed me to be his servant.
He made my words as sharp as a sword.
With his own hand he protected me.
He made me like an arrow,
sharp and ready for use.
He said to me, "You are my servant;
because of you, people will praise me.
I will make you a light to the nations—
so that all the world may be saved."

Glory to the Father, and to the Son, and to the
    Holy Spirit:
as it was in the beginning, is now, and will be for
    ever. Amen.

Prayer

O God of all the nations of the earth:
Remember the multitudes who have been created
    in your image
but have not known the redeeming work of our
    Savior Jesus Christ;
and grant that, by the prayers and labors of your
    holy Church,
they may be brought to know and worship you
as you have been revealed in your Son;
who lives and reigns with you and the Holy Spirit,
one God, for ever and ever.
Amen.

Blessing

May the Son of God, who has given us
understanding,
† bless us and keep us.
Amen.

DAY 11

Parables of the Kingdom of God

Jesus is the Messenger "bringing Good News, the news of peace." Beginning with simple stories familiar to all, he leads his hearers step by step to the Word of God which is alive, active and sharper than a sword. "Blessed are they who hear and believe."

Come, let us worship the Lord.
He proclaims the Good News.

Psalm 92: Praise God for the Gospel
Antiphon: I sing for joy because of your mighty deeds.

How good it is to give thanks to you, O Lord,
to sing in your honor, O Most High God,
to proclaim your constant love every morning
and your faithfulness every night,
with the music of stringed instruments
and with melody on the harp.
Your mighty deeds, O Lord, make me glad;
because of what you have done, I sing for joy.

How great are your actions, Lord!
How deep are your thoughts!
This is something a fool cannot know,
a stupid man cannot understand;
the wicked may grow like weeds,
those who do wrong may prosper;
yet they will be totally destroyed,
because you, Lord, are supreme for ever.

The righteous will flourish like palm trees;
they will grow like the cedars of Lebanon.
They are like trees planted in the house of the
    Lord,
that flourish in the Temple of our God,
that still bear fruit in old age
and are always green and strong.
This shows that the Lord is just,
that there is no wrong in my protector.

Glory to the Father, and to the Son, and to the
    Holy Spirit:
as it was in the beginning, is now, and will be for
    ever. Amen.

Prayer
Lord Jesus Christ, eternal Word of God,
help us rejoice in your mighty deeds
and flourish in your gracious presence,
as we await your return in glory
to judge the living and the dead.
Blessed are you for ever.
Amen.

A Reading from the Letter to the Hebrews (4:12–13)

The word of God is alive and active, sharper than any double-edged sword. It cuts all the way through, to where soul and spirit meet, to where joints and marrow come together. It judges the thoughts and desires of the heart. There is nothing that can be hid from God; everything in all creation is exposed and lies open before his eyes. And it is to him that we must all give an account of ourselves.

Responsory

The Word was made flesh and dwelt among us.
The Word was made flesh and dwelt among us.
A sharp two-edged sword came out of his mouth.
The Word was made flesh and dwelt among us.
Glory to the Father, and to the Son, and to the
    Holy Spirit.
The Word was made flesh and dwelt among us.

A Reading from the Good News according to St. Mark (4:1–2, 30–34)

Jesus began to teach beside Lake Galilee. The crowd that gathered around him was so large that he got into a boat and sat in it. The boat was out in the water, and the crowd stood on the shore at the water's edge. "What shall we say the Kingdom of God is like?" asked Jesus. "What parable shall we use to explain it? It is like this. A man takes a mustard seed, the smallest seed in the world, and plants it in the ground. After a while it grows up and becomes the biggest of all plants. It puts out such large branches that the birds come and make their nests in the shade."

Jesus preached his message to the people, using many other parables like these; he told them as much as they could understand. He would not speak to them without using parables.

The Spirit of the Lord has chosen me.
To bring Good News to the poor.

Canticle of Isaiah (52:7–8, 10): The Good News of Peace

Antiphon: Preach the Good News to all creation.

How wonderful it is to see
a messenger coming across the mountains,
bringing good news, the news of peace.
He announces the victory and says to Zion,
"Your God is king!"

Those who guard the city are shouting,
shouting together for joy.
They can see with their own eyes
the return of the Lord to Zion.

The Lord will use his holy power;
he will save his people,
and all the world will see it.

Glory to the Father, and to the Son, and to the
    Holy Spirit:
as it was in the beginning, is now, and will be for
    ever. Amen.

Prayer
Lord Jesus Christ, Son of the living God,
illumine the world with the radiance of your glory
and the splendor of your saving message,
that all nations may acknowledge you as their
    only Savior;
for you live and reign for ever and ever.
Amen.

Blessing
May God, the only God,
who saves us through Jesus Christ our Lord,
† bless us and keep us.
Amen.

DAY 12

Jesus: Messiah and Lord

Little by little, as they watch and listen to him, the disciples of Jesus come to recognize him as he truly is: the fulfillment of ancient prophecy, the Anointed of YHWH, the King, Priest and Prophet of the new Israel.

Come, let us adore Christ, the Son of the living God.
For he is our light and our salvation.

Psalm 110: King, Priest and Conqueror
Antiphon: You are my Son; today I have become your Father.

The Lord said to my lord, the king,
"Sit here at my right side
until I put your enemies under your feet."
From Zion the Lord will extend your royal power.
"Rule over your enemies," he says.
On the day you fight your enemies,
your people will volunteer.
Like the dew of early morning
your young men will come to you on the sacred hills.

71

The Lord made a solemn promise
and will not take it back:
"You will be a priest forever
in the line of succession to Melchizedek."

The Lord is at your right side;
when he becomes angry,
he will defeat kings.
He will pass judgment on the nations
and fill the battlefield with corpses;
he will defeat kings all over the earth.
The king will drink from the stream by the road,
and strengthened, he will stand victorious.

Glory to the Father, and to the Son, and to the
    Holy Spirit:
as it was in the beginning, is now, and will be for
    ever. Amen.

Prayer
Lord Jesus Christ,
faithful witness and first-born from the dead,
ruler of the kings of the earth,
wash away our sins in your blood
and make us a line of kings and priests
to serve your God and Father,
now and for ever.
Amen.

A Reading from the Letter of Paul the Apostle to the Colossians (1:15–18)
Christ is the visible likeness of the invisible God.
He is the first-born Son, superior to all created

things. For through him God created everything in heaven and on earth, the seen and the unseen things, including spiritual powers, lords, rulers and authorities. God created the whole universe through him and for him. Christ existed before all things, and in union with him all things have their proper place. He is the first-born Son, who was raised from death, in order that he alone might have the first place in all things.

Responsory

Christ must reign until God puts all enemies under his feet.

Christ must reign until God puts all enemies under his feet.

He is the King of kings and the Lord of lords.

Christ must reign until God puts all enemies under his feet.

Glory to the Father, and to the Son, and to the Holy Spirit.

Christ must reign until God puts all enemies under his feet.

A Reading from the Good News according to St. Mark (8:27–33)

Jesus and his disciples went away to the villages near Caesarea Philippi. On the way he asked them, "Tell me, who do people say I am?" "Some say that you are John the Baptist," they answered; "others say that you are Elijah, while others say that you are one of the prophets." "What about

you?'' he asked them. ''Who do you say I am?''
Peter answered, ''You are the Messiah.''

Jesus Christ is the same.
Yesterday, today and for ever.

Canticle of Mary (Luke 1:46–55)
*Antiphon: Christ is victor; Christ is ruler, Christ is
Lord of all.*

My soul proclaims the greatness of the Lord;
my spirit rejoices in God my Savior
for he has looked with favor on his lowly servant.

From this day all generations will call me blessed:
the Almighty has done great things for me,
and holy is his name.

He has mercy on those who fear him
in every generation.
He has shown the strength of his arm,
he has scattered the proud in their conceit.

He has cast down the mighty from their thrones,
and has lifted up the lowly.
He has filled the hungry with good things,
and the rich he has sent away empty.

He has come to the help of his servant Israel
for he has remembered his promise of mercy,

the promise he made to our ancestors,
to Abraham and Sarah and their children for ever.

Glory to the Father, and to the Son, and to the
    Holy Spirit:
as it was in the beginning, is now, and will be for
    ever. Amen.

Prayer

Almighty and merciful God,
you break the power of evil
and make all things new
in your Son Jesus Christ, the King of the universe.
May all in heaven and earth acclaim your glory
and never cease to praise you.
We ask this through Christ our Lord.
Amen.

Blessing

May Christ Jesus, God's anointed,
† bless us and keep us.
Amen.

DAY 13

Jesus: God's Suffering Servant

As Simon Peter recognized, Jesus is the true Messiah of Israel but he is also the Suffering Servant of God depicted in Isaiah; he is "the Lamb of God who takes away the sin of the world," the obedient Servant of God who "became the source of eternal salvation for all those who obey him."

Come, let us adore Christ the Lord.
He endured suffering and temptation for our sake.

Psalm 54: Jesus Prays To Be Delivered from Enemies
Antiphon: Into your hands I commend my spirit.

Save me by your power, O God;
set me free by your might!
Hear my prayer, O God;
listen to my words!

Proud men are coming to attack me;
cruel men are trying to kill me—
men who do not care about God.

But God is my helper.
The Lord is my defender.
May God use their own evil
to punish my enemies.
He will destroy them
because he is faithful.
I will gladly offer you sacrifice, O Lord;
I will give you thanks
because you are good.
You have rescued me from all my troubles,
and I have seen my enemies defeated.

Glory to the Father, and to the Son, and to the
    Holy Spirit:
as it was in the beginning, is now, and will be for
    ever. Amen.

Prayer
Father of mercies,
look upon this family of yours
for which our Lord Jesus Christ did not hesitate
to hand himself over to sinners
and to undergo the torment of the cross;
he lives and reigns with you and the Holy Spirit,
one God, now and for ever.
Amen.

A Reading from the Letter to the Hebrews (5:7–10)
In his life on earth Jesus made his prayers and
requests with loud cries and tears to God, who
could save him from death. Because he was

humble and devoted, God heard him. But even though he was God's Son, he learned through his sufferings to be obedient. When he was made perfect, he became the source of eternal salvation for all those who obey him, and God declared him to be high priest, as the successor of Melchizedeck.

Responsory
Let us glory in the cross of our Lord Jesus Christ.
Let us glory in the cross of our Lord Jesus Christ.
For in him is our salvation, life and resurrection.
Let us glory in the cross of our Lord Jesus Christ.
Glory to the Father, and to the Son, and to the
    Holy Spirit.
Let us glory in the cross of our Lord Jesus Christ.

A Reading from the Good News according to St. Mark (8:31–33)
Then Jesus began to teach his disciples: ''The Son of Man must suffer much and be rejected by the elders, the chief priests, and the teachers of the Law. He will be put to death, but three days later he will rise to life.'' He made this very clear to them. So Peter took him aside and began to rebuke him. But Jesus turned around, looked at his disciples, and rebuked Peter. ''Get away from me, Satan,'' he said. ''Your thoughts don't come from God but from man.''

Christ became obedient unto death.
Even to death on a cross.

Canticle of the Lamb (Rev. 4:11; 5:9, 10, 12)

*Antiphon: Jesus is the Lamb of God who takes
away the sin of the world.*

Worthy are you, our Lord and God,
to receive glory and honor and power.
For you created all things
and by your will they existed and were created.

Worthy are you, O Lord,
to take the scroll and to open its seals.
For you were slain
and by your blood you ransomed us for God
from every tribe and tongue and people and
    nation.
You have made us a kingdom and priests to our
    God,
and we shall reign on the earth.

Worthy is the Lamb who was slain
to receive power and wealth and wisdom and
    might
and honor and glory and blessing.

Glory to the Father, and to the Son, and to the
    Holy Spirit:
as it was in the beginning, is now, and will be for
    ever. Amen.

Prayer
By the power of your cross, O Lord,
set us free from all our sins,

save us in the time of trial
and raise us up on the great and final day.
You live and reign for ever and ever.
Amen.

Blessing
May the glorious passion of our Lord Jesus Christ
† bring us to the joys of paradise.
Amen.

DAY 14

Jesus Is Transfigured on Mount Tabor

Although he is the Suffering Servant, Jesus is also the King of Glory predicted by the Law and the Prophets (Moses and Elijah), acknowledged by the Father as his "own dear Son" and revealed on the holy mountain to his confused disciples.

Come, let us worship the King of glory.
He outshines every constellation of the stars.

Psalm 45: The Royal Bridegroom
Antiphon: God's glory shines in the face of Christ.

You are the most handsome of men;
you are an eloquent speaker.
God has always blessed you.
Buckle on your sword, mighty king;
you are glorious and majestic.

Ride on in majesty to victory
for the defense of truth and justice!
Your strength will win you great victories!
Your arrows are sharp,
they pierce the hearts of your enemies;
nations fall down at your feet.

The kingdom that God has given you
will last forever and ever.
You rule over your people with justice;
you love what is right and hate what is evil.
That is why God, your God, has chosen you
and has poured out more happiness on you
than on any other king.

Glory to the Father, and to the Son, and to the
    Holy Spirit:
as it was in the beginning, is now, and will be for
    ever. Amen.

Prayer

At the time of your transfiguration on the mount,
O Lord of glory,
you showed your disciples as much of your
    splendor
as they could endure.
In your kindness,
make of us heirs of the Kingdom with you
and sharers in the glory that is to come.
You live and reign with the Father and the Holy
    Spirit,
one God, now and for ever.
Amen.

A Reading from the Second Letter of
St. Peter the Apostle (1:16–18)

We have not depended on made-up stories in
making known to you the mighty coming of our
Lord Jesus Christ. With our own eyes we saw his

greatness. We were there when he was given honor and glory by God the Father, when the voice came to him from the Supreme Glory, saying, "This is my own dear Son, with whom I am pleased!" We ourselves heard this voice coming from heaven, when we were with him on the holy mountain.

Responsory
Jesus will change our weak mortal bodies.
Jesus will change our weak mortal bodies.
And make them like his own glorious body.
Jesus will change our weak mortal bodies.
Glory to the Father, and to the Son, and to the
    Holy Spirit.
Jesus will change our weak mortal bodies.

A Reading from the Good News according to St. Mark (9:2–4, 7–9)
Six days later Jesus took with him Peter, James and John, and led them up a high mountain, where they were alone. As they looked on, a change came over Jesus, and his clothes became shining white—whiter than anyone in the world could wash them. Then the three disciples saw Elijah and Moses talking with Jesus. Then a cloud appeared and covered them with its shadow, and a voice came from the cloud, "This is my own dear Son—listen to him!" As they came down from the mountain, Jesus ordered them, "Don't tell anyone what you have seen, until the Son of Man has risen from death."

All of us reflect the glory of the Lord.
With uncovered faces!

Canticle: A Cento of Psalm 89
Antiphon: You, O Christ, are the King of glory!

O Lord, I will always sing of your constant love;
I will proclaim your faithfulness forever.
I know that your love will last for all time,
that your faithfulness is as permanent as the sky.

The heavens sing of the wonderful things you do;
they sing of your faithfulness, Lord.
No one in heaven is like you, Lord;
none of the heavenly beings is your equal;
they all stand in awe of you.

Heaven is yours, the earth also;
you made the world and everything in it.
You created the north and the south;
Mount Tabor and Mount Hermon sing to you for
joy.

Happy are the people who worship you with
songs,
who live in the light of your kindness!
Because of you they rejoice all day long,
and they praise you for your goodness.

Glory to the Father, and to the Son, and to the
Holy Spirit:
as it was in the beginning, is now, and will be for
ever. Amen.

Prayer
God our Father,
in the transfigured glory of Christ your Son,
you strengthen our faith
by confirming the witness of your prophets,
and show us the splendor of your beloved sons
        and daughters.
As we listen to the voice of your Son,
help us to become heirs of eternal life with him
who lives and reigns with you and the Holy Spirit,
one God, for ever and ever.
Amen.

Blessing
May the King of glory, whose face shines like the
        sun,
† bless us and keep us.
Amen.

DAY 15

Jesus Raises Lazarus from the Dead

Jesus, the King of Glory, the Transfigured One of Tabor, illumines the darkness of the tomb, looses Lazarus from the bonds of death and reveals himself as the Resurrection and the Life. "Whoever lives and believes in me will never die."

Come, let us adore the Lord of glory.
He is our life and our resurrection.

Psalm 30: Lazarus Thanks His Savior
Antiphon: May the light of your face shine upon us, O Christ.

I praise you, Lord, because you have saved me
and kept my enemies from gloating over me.
I cried to you for help, O Lord my God,
and you healed me;
you kept me from the grave.
I was on my way to the depths below,
but you restored my life.

Sing praise to the Lord,
all his faithful people!

Remember what the Holy One has done,
and give him thanks!
Tears may flow in the night,
but joy comes in the morning.

I called to you, Lord;
I begged for your help:
"What will you gain from my death?
What profit from my going to the grave?
Are dead people able to praise you?
Can they proclaim your unfailing goodness?"
Help me, Lord, and be merciful!
Help me, Lord!

You have changed my sadness into a joyful
        dance;
you have taken away my sorrow
and surrounded me with joy.
So I will not be silent;
I will sing praise to you.
Lord, you are my God;
I will give you thanks for ever.

Glory to the Father, and to the Son, and to the
        Holy Spirit:
as it was in the beginning, is now, and will be for
        ever. Amen.

Prayer
O Christ our Lord,
when you raised Lazarus from the dead
before the time of your passion,

you sealed the future resurrection of us all.
In your great generosity,
rescue us from sin, death and hell
and bring us in safety to the haven of peace,
where you live and reign, now and for ever.
Amen.

A Reading from St. Paul's Letter to the Romans (8:11)

If the Spirit of God, who raised Jesus from death, lives in you, then he who raised Christ from death will also give life to your mortal bodies by the presence of his Spirit in you.

Responsory

Jesus Christ is the same, yesterday, today and for
 ever.
Jesus Christ is the same, yesterday, today and for
 ever.
If we die with Christ, we shall live with Christ.
Jesus Christ is the same, yesterday, today and for
 ever.
Glory to the Father, and to the Son, and to the
 Holy Spirit.
Jesus Christ is the same, yesterday, today and for
 ever.

A Reading from the Good News according to St. John (11:38–44)

Deeply moved, Jesus went to the tomb which was a cave with a stone placed at the entrance. "Take the stone away!" Jesus ordered. Martha, the dead man's sister, answered, "There will be a bad smell, Lord. He has been buried four days." Jesus said to her, "Didn't I tell you that you would see God's glory if you believed?" They took the stone away. Jesus looked up and said, "I thank you, Father, that you listen to me. I know that you always listen to me, but I say this for the sake of the people here, so that they will believe that you sent me." After he had said this, he called out in a loud voice, "Lazarus, come out!" He came out, his hands and feet wrapped in grave cloths, and with a cloth around his face. "Untie him," Jesus told them, "and let him go."

Many of the people saw what Jesus did.
And they believed in him.

Canticle of Zachary (Luke 1:68–79)
Antiphon: I am the resurrection and the life.
Whoever lives and believes in me will
never die.

Blessed be the Lord, the God of Israel;
he has come to his people and set them free.
He has raised up for us a mighty savior,
born of the house of his servant David.

Through his holy prophets he promised of old
that he would save us from our enemies,
from the hands of all who hate us.

This was the oath he swore to our father Abraham:
to set us free from the hands of our enemies,

free to worship him without fear,
holy and righteous in his sight
all the days of our life.

You, my child, shall be called the prophet of the
    Most High;
for you will go before the Lord to prepare his way,
to give his people knowledge of salvation
by the forgiveness of their sins.

In the tender compassion of our God
the dawn from on high shall break upon us,
to shine on those who dwell in darkness and the
    shadow of death,
and to guide our feet into the way of peace.

Glory to the Father, and to the Son, and to the
    Holy Spirit:
as it was in the beginning, is now, and will be for
    ever. Amen.

Prayer

We thank you, heavenly Father,
that you have delivered us from the dominion of
    sin and death
and brought us into the kingdom of your Son;
and we pray that, as by his death he has recalled
    us to life,
so by his love he may raise us to eternal joys;
who lives and reigns with you,
in the unity of the Holy Spirit,
one God, now and for ever.
Amen.

Blessing

May Christ, the first-fruits of those who fall asleep
    in death,
† bless us and keep us.
Amen.

DAY 16

Jesus Enters Jerusalem in Triumph

Before a week of rejection by the rich and powerful of this world, Jesus has a day of acceptance by the meek and lowly. As it was at his birth, so it is at the hour of his death. Then angels sang: "Glory to God in the highest!" Now children sing: "Hosanna in the highest!"

Come, let us adore Christ our Lord.
Who suffered for our salvation.

Canticle of Zechariah (9:9–10):
The Prince of Peace
Antiphon: Hosanna to the Son of David!

Rejoice, rejoice, people of Zion!
Shout for joy, you people of Jerusalem!
Look, your king is coming to you!
He comes triumphant and victorious,
but humble and riding on a donkey—
on a colt, the foal of a donkey.

The Lord says,
"I will remove the war chariots from Israel
and take the horses from Jerusalem;
the bows used in battle will be destroyed.

Your king will make peace among the nations;
he will rule from sea to sea,
from the river to the ends of the earth.''

Glory to the Father, and to the Son, and to the
    Holy Spirit:
as it was in the beginning, is now, and will be for
    ever. Amen.

Prayer
Lord our God,
you sent your only Son
to save the world by his blessed passion;
when he entered Jerusalem,
the people waved branches of palm and olive
in token of his coming resurrection.
As we too cry, ''Hosanna in the highest!''
protect us as we await the life-giving resurrection
of our Lord and Savior Jesus Christ;
he lives and reigns with you and the Holy Spirit,
now and for ever.
Amen.

A Reading from the Prophet Isaiah (62:11)
Tell the people of Jerusalem that the Lord is
coming to save you, bringing with him the people
he has rescued. You will be called ''God's Holy
People,'' ''The People the Lord Has Saved.''
Jerusalem will be called ''The City That God
Loves,'' ''The City That God Did Not Forsake.''

Responsory
You redeemed us, O Lord, with your blood.
You redeemed us, O Lord, with your blood.
From every family, language, people and nation.
You redeemed us, O Lord, with your blood.
Glory to the Father, and to the Son, and to the
　　Holy Spirit.
You redeemed us, O Lord, with your blood.

A Reading from the Good News according to St. Mark (11:7–11)

His disciples brought the colt to Jesus, threw their cloaks over the animal, and Jesus got on. Many people spread their cloaks on the road, while others cut branches in the field and spread them on the road. The people who were in front and those who followed behind began to shout, "Praise God! God bless him who comes in the name of the Lord! God bless the coming kingdom of King David our father! Praise be to God!"

The children of Jerusalem welcomed Christ as
　　king.
Hosanna in the highest!

Hymn for Palm Sunday

All glory, laud and honor
To you, Redeemer King,
To whom the lips of children
Made sweet hosannas ring.

You are the King of Israel
And David's royal Son,

Now in the Lord's Name coming,
Our King and Blessed One.

The multitude of pilgrims
With palms before you went,
Our praise and prayer and anthems
Before you we present.

To you before your passion
They sang their hymns of praise.
To you, now high exalted,
Our melody we raise.

All glory, laud and honor
To you, Redeemer King,
To whom the lips of children
Made sweet hosannas ring.

Prayer
In company with the angels and the believing
        children,
let us acclaim death's Conqueror
with the cry:
Hosanna in the highest!
By the power of your glorious and life-giving
        cross,
O Lord,
bring the wickedness of the Evil One to nothing
and stretch forth your right hand

to protect those whom you have redeemed,
you who live and reign with the Father and the
      Holy Spirit,
now and for ever.
Amen.

Blessing
May the glorious passion of our Lord Jesus Christ
† bring us to the joys of paradise.
Amen.

DAY 17

The Cleansing of the Temple

At his presentation in the Temple, old Simeon had predicted that Jesus would be a "sign of contradiction." When he comes again to the Temple, "his own received him not" (Jn 1:11). "Life and death are set before us, whichever we choose shall be given us" (Sir 15:17).

Come, let us adore Christ the Lord.
He comes to prepare a people for God.

Canticle of Zechariah (13:7–9):
Jesus Tests and Purifies
Antiphon: The Lord will visit his people.

Awake, sword, against my shepherd
and against the man who is my companion—
It is Yahweh Sabaoth who speaks.
I am going to strike the shepherd
so that the sheep may be scattered,
and I will turn my hand against the weak.
And it will happen throughout this territory—
it is Yahweh who speaks—
that two-thirds of it will be cut off

and the remaining third will be left.
I will lead that third into the fire,
and refine them as silver is refined,
test them as gold is tested.
They will call on my name
and I shall listen;
and I shall say: "These are my people,"
and each will say: "Yahweh is my God!"

Glory to the Father, and to the Son, and to the
    Holy Spirit:
as it was in the beginning, is now, and will be for
    ever. Amen.

Prayer
Holy God,
your Son came to the temple of Jerusalem
to purify, restore and replace it.
Raise up a people for yourself,
purified and tested in the fire of affliction
and ever ready to do your will.
Through the same Christ our Lord.
Amen.

A Reading from the Prophet Malachi (3:1–3)
The Lord Almighty answers, "I will send my
messenger to prepare the way for me. Then the
Lord you are looking for will suddenly come to his
Temple. The messenger you long to see will come
and proclaim my covenant. But who will be able
to endure when he comes? Who will be able to
survive when he appears? He will be like strong

soap, like a fire that refines metal. He will come to judge like one who refines and purifies silver."

Responsory
They will look at him whom they pierced.
They will look at him whom they pierced.
They will mourn for him like an only child.
They will look at him whom they pierced.
Glory to the Father, and to the Son, and to the
     Holy Spirit.
They will look at him whom they pierced.

A Reading from the Good News according to St. Mark (11:15–18)
When they arrived in Jerusalem, Jesus went to the Temple and began to drive out all those who were buying and selling. He overturned the tables of the money changers and the stools of those who sold pigeons, and he would not let anyone carry anything through the Temple courtyards. He then taught the people: "It is written in the Scriptures that God said, 'My Temple will be called a house of prayer for the people of all nations.' But you have turned it into a hideout for thieves." The chief priests and the teachers of the Law heard of this, so they began looking for some way to kill Jesus. They were afraid of him, because the whole crowd was amazed at his teaching.

My devotion to your house, O God.
Burns in me like a fire.

Canticle of Zephaniah (3:14–18)
Antiphon: The Lord is in our midst.

Shout for joy, daughter of Zion,
Israel, shout aloud!
Rejoice, exult with all your heart,
daughter of Jerusalem!
The Lord has repealed your sentence;
he has driven your enemies away.
The Lord, the king of Israel, is in your midst;
you have no more evil to fear.

When that day comes, word will come to
    Jerusalem:
Zion, have no fear,
do not let your hands fall limp.
The Lord your God is in your midst,
a victorious warrior.
He will exult with joy over you,
he will renew you by his love;
he will dance with shouts of joy for you
as on a day of festival.

Glory to the Father, and to the Son, and to the
    Holy Spirit:
as it was in the beginning, is now, and will be for
    ever. Amen.

Prayer
Come, Lord Jesus,
and visit your people in peace.

Give us fresh courage
and raise us to the joy of your kingdom.
Blessed are you forever.
Amen.

Blessing
May Christ Jesus, who loved us and washed away
our sins in his blood,
† bless us and keep us.
Amen.

DAY 18

Mary Anoints Jesus in Preparation for His Burial

God's wisdom is displayed in Mary; as a "friend of God" she becomes a prophet, symbolically preparing Jesus' body for burial. To a counterpoint of complaint, Jesus answers: "She has done a fine and beautiful thing for me." We still tell the story "in memory of her."

Come, let us adore Christ the Lord.
He suffered for our salvation.

In Praise of Wisdom (7:25–8:1):
A Wise and Valiant Woman
Antiphon: She has done a fine and beautiful thing for me.

Wisdom is a breath of the power of God,
pure emanation of the glory of the Almighty;
hence nothing impure can find a way into her.
She is a reflection of the eternal light,
untarnished mirror of God's active power,
image of his goodness.

Although alone, she can do all;
herself unchanging, she makes all things new.
In each generation she passes into holy souls,
she makes them friends of God and prophets;
for God loves only the one who lives with
    Wisdom.
She is indeed more splendid than the sun,
she outshines all the constellations;
compared with light, she takes first place,
for light must yield to light,
but over Wisdom evil can never triumph.
She deploys her strength from one end of the earth
    to the other,
ordering all things for good.

Glory to the Father, and to the Son, and to the
    Holy Spirit:
as it was in the beginning, is now, and will be for
    ever. Amen.

Prayer
Lord Jesus Christ,
you loved us and delivered yourself up for us
as an agreeable and fragrant sacrifice to God;
rescue us from our former darkness
and teach us to walk as children of the light
in all goodness, justice and truth.
You live and reign for ever and ever.
Amen.

A Reading from the First Letter of St. John (4:7–10)

Dear friends, let us love one another, because love comes from God. Whoever loves is a child of God and knows God. Whoever does not love does not know God, for God is love. And God showed his love for us by sending his only Son into the world, so that we might have life through him. This is what love is: it is not that we have loved God, but that he loved us and sent his Son to be the means by which our sins are forgiven.

Responsory

The Son of Man will be handed over to those who will kill him.

The Son of Man will be handed over to those who will kill him.

Three days later he will rise to life.

The Son of Man will be handed over to those who will kill him.

Glory to the Father, and to the Son, and to the Holy Spirit.

The Son of Man will be handed over to those who will kill him.

A Reading from the Good News according to St. Mark (14:3–9)

Jesus was in Bethany at the house of Simon, a man who had suffered from a dreaded skin disease. While Jesus was eating, a woman came in with an alabaster jar full of a very expensive perfume made of pure nard. She broke the jar and poured the perfume on Jesus' head. Some of the people there became angry and said to one another, "What was the use of wasting the perfume? It could have been sold for more than three hundred silver coins and the money given to the poor!" And they criticized her harshly. But Jesus said, "Leave her alone! Why are you bothering her? She has done a fine and beautiful thing for me. You will always have poor people with you, and any time you want to, you can help them. But you will not always have me. She did what she could; she poured perfume on my body to prepare it ahead of time for burial. Now, I assure you that wherever the gospel is preached all over the world, what she has done will be told in memory of her."

The sweet smell of perfume.
Filled the whole house.

Canticle of Mary (Luke 1:46–55)
Antiphon: What she has done will be told in memory of her.

My soul proclaims the greatness of the Lord;
my spirit rejoices in God my Savior
for he has looked with favor on his lowly servant.

From this day all generations will call me blessed:
the Almighty has done great things for me,
and holy is his name.

He has mercy on those who fear him
in every generation.
He has shown the strength of his arm,
he has scattered the proud in their conceit.

He has cast down the mighty from their thrones,
and has lifted up the lowly.
He has filled the hungry with good things,
and the rich he has sent away empty.

He has come to the help of his servant Israel
for he has remembered his promise of mercy,
the promise he made to our ancestors,
to Abraham and Sarah and their children for ever.

Glory to the Father, and to the Son, and to the
    Holy Spirit:
as it was in the beginning, is now, and will be for
    ever. Amen.

Prayer
Gracious Father,
as we venerate the passion, death and resurrection
of our Lord, God and Savior Jesus Christ,
may the unmistakable perfume of his abiding
    presence
be the fresh fragrance of life itself for us,
now and for ever.
Amen.

106

Blessing
May the glorious passion of our Lord Jesus Christ
† bring us to the joys of paradise.
Amen.

DAY 19

The Last Supper

Jesus is God-with-us, God-for-us, yesterday, today and for ever. As we eat and drink in his memory, we fulfill the promise made to our ancestors and receive a "pledge of the glory which is to come." "The Lord does not let us forget his wonderful actions."

Come, let us adore Christ, the bread of life.
Come, let us adore him.

Hymn
Hail our Savior's glorious Body,
Which his Virgin Mother bore;
Hail the Blood which, shed for sinners,
Did a broken world restore;
Hail the sacrament most holy,
Flesh and Blood of Christ adore!

Come, adore this wondrous presence;
Bow to Christ, the source of grace!
Here is kept the ancient promise
Of God's earthly dwelling place!
Sight is blind before God's glory,
Faith alone may see his face!

Glory be to God the Father,
Praise to his co-equal Son,
Adoration to the Spirit,
Bond of love, in Godhead one!
Blest be God by all creation
Joyously while ages run.

Pange Lingua Gloriosi

Psalm 111: A Memorial Meal of God's Wonderful Actions

*Antiphon: Our kind and merciful Lord never
forgets his covenant.*

With all my heart I will thank the Lord,
in the assembly of his people.
How wonderful are the things the Lord does!
All who are delighted with them
want to understand them.
All he does is full of honor and majesty;
his righteousness is eternal.

The Lord does not let us forget his wonderful
        actions;
he is kind and merciful.
He provides food for those who fear him;
he never forgets his covenant.
He has shown his power to his people,
by giving them the lands of foreigners.

In all he does he is faithful and just;
all his commandments are dependable.

They last for all time;
they were given in truth and righteousness.

He set his people free
and made an eternal covenant with them.
Holy and mighty is he!

The way to become wise is to fear the Lord;
he gives sound judgment to all who obey his
     commands.
He is to be praised for ever.

Glory to the Father, and to the Son, and to the
     Holy Spirit:
as it was in the beginning, is now, and will be for
     ever. Amen.

Prayer
Kind and merciful Lord,
in the wonderful sacrament of the altar
you give us a living memorial of your dying and
     rising
and of the everlasting covenant established in
     your blood.
Keep us ever mindful of your wonderful actions
and faithful to your dependable commandments.
You live and reign for ever and ever.
Amen.

**A Reading from the First Letter of Paul the
Apostle to the Corinthians (10:16–17)**
The cup of blessing for which we give thanks to
God: do we not share in the blood of Christ when

we drink from this cup? And the bread we break: do we not share in the body of Christ when we eat this bread? Because there is the one bread, all of us, though many, are one body, because we all share the same loaf.

Responsory
The Lord gave them bread from heaven.
The Lord gave them bread from heaven.
Sending down manna for them to eat.
The Lord gave them bread from heaven.
Glory to the Father, and to the Son, and to the
   Holy Spirit.
The Lord gave them bread from heaven.

A Reading from the Good News according to St. Mark (14:22–26)
While they were eating, Jesus took a piece of bread, gave a prayer of thanks, broke it, and gave it to his disciples. "Take it," he said, "this is my body." Then he took a cup, gave thanks to God, and handed it to them; and they all drank from it. Jesus said, "This is my blood which is poured out for many, my blood which seals God's covenant. I tell you, I will never again drink this wine until the day I drink the new wine in the Kingdom of God."

Come, and eat my bread.
Drink the wine I have prepared for you.

Canticle of The Blessed Sacrament (John 6)

Antiphon: How sacred is the feast in which Christ
is our food,
the memorial of his passion is
celebrated anew,
our hearts are filled with grace,
and we are given a pledge of the
glory which is to come.

I am the bread of life;
whoever comes to me will never hunger,
whoever believes in me will never thirst.
I am the living bread that has come down from
    heaven;
no one who eats of it will ever die.
Anyone who eats of this bread,
will live for ever.
The bread that I give is my flesh
for the life of the world.

Unless you eat the flesh of the Son of Man
and drink his blood,
you will have no life in you.
Those who eat my flesh and drink my blood
are in possession of eternal life;
and I will raise them up on the last day.

My flesh is real food
and my blood is real drink.
Those who eat my flesh and drink my blood
are united with me,
and I am united with them.

Whoever eats me will live because of me.
This is the bread that has come down from
    heaven.

Glory to the Father, and to the Son, and to the
    Holy Spirit:
as it was in the beginning, is now, and will be for
    ever. Amen.

Prayer
Lord Jesus Christ,
you gave us the Eucharist
as the memorial of your suffering and death.
May our worship of this sacrament of your body
    and blood
help us to know the salvation you won for us
and the peace of the kingdom
where you live with the Father and the Holy
    Spirit,
one God, for ever and ever.
Amen.

Blessing
May Christ, the bread of life,
† be our strength and stay.
Amen.

DAY 20

Jesus in the Garden of Gethsemane

Peter, James and John were with Jesus on the holy
mountain when he was transfigured; they are with
him now in his hour of agony. As he sweats blood,
they sleep.

Come, let us adore Christ our Lord.
He was sorrowful even unto death.

Canticle of Isaiah (12:1–3): God Is My Savior!
*Antiphon: The Lord remembers his promise of
mercy.*

I praise you, Lord!
You were angry with me,
but now you comfort me
and are angry no longer.

God is my savior;
I will trust him and not be afraid.
The Lord gives me power and strength;
he is my savior.
As fresh water brings joy to the thirsty,
so God's people rejoice
when he saves them.

Glory to the Father, and to the Son, and to the
    Holy Spirit:
as it was in the beginning, is now, and will be for
    ever. Amen.

Prayer
Lord Jesus Christ,
when we are overwhelmed by trials and
    temptations,
protect us under the shadow of your cross,
while we await in sure and certain hope
the full revelation of your victory over death and
    hell.
You live and reign for ever and ever.
Amen.

A Reading from the Book of Wisdom (2:18–20)
If the virtuous man is God's son, God will take his
part and rescue him from the clutches of his
enemies. Let us test him with cruelty and with
torture, and thus explore this gentleness of his and
put his endurance to the proof. Let us condemn
him to shameful death since he will be looked
after—we have his word for it.

Responsory
My soul is sorrowful even unto death.
My soul is sorrowful even unto death.
Watch and pray; the spirit is willing but the flesh
    is weak.
My soul is sorrowful even unto death.

Glory to the Father, and to the Son, and to the
Holy Spirit.
My soul is sorrowful even unto death.

A Reading from the Good News according to St. Mark (14:32–36)

They came to a place called Gethsemane, and
Jesus said to his disciples, "Sit here while I pray."
He took Peter, James and John with him. Distress
and anguish came over him, and he said to them,
"The sorrow in my heart is so great that it almost
crushes me. Stay here and keep watch." He went
a little farther on, threw himself on the ground,
and prayed, if possible, he might not have to go
through that time of suffering. "Father," he
prayed. "My Father! All things are possible for
you. Take this cup of suffering away from me. Yet
not what I want, but what you want."

The hour has come!
The Son of Man is being handed over to sinners.

Canticle of Isaiah (5:1–2)

Antiphon: My people, what have I done to you?
How have I offended you? Answer me!

Listen while I sing you this song,
a song of my friend and his vineyard:
My friend had a vineyard
on a very fertile hill.
He dug the soil and cleared it of stones;
he planted the finest vines.

116

He built a tower to guard them,
dug a pit for treading the grapes.
He waited for the grapes to ripen,
but every grape was sour.

Israel is the vineyard of the Lord Almighty;
the people of Judah are the vines he planted.
He expected them to do what was good,
but instead they committed murder.
He expected them to do what was right,
but their victims cried out for justice.

Glory to the Father, and to the Son, and to the
    Holy Spirit:
as it was in the beginning, is now, and will be for
    ever. Amen.

Prayer
Lord, by shedding his blood for us,
your Son, Jesus Christ,
established the paschal mystery.
In your goodness, make us holy
and watch over us always.
We ask this through Christ our Lord.
Amen.

Blessing
May the Man of Sorrows, afflicted with grief,
✝ bless us and keep us.
Amen.

DAY 21

The Kiss of Judas

Most of Jesus' disciples misunderstood him; his chosen three slept during his agony in the garden; one actively betrayed him—and with a kiss!

Come, let us worship Christ our Savior.
He was betrayed into the hands of sinners.

Psalm 109: Jesus Prays in the Face of His Betrayers

Antiphon: Judas was looking for a chance to betray him.

I praise you, God; don't remain silent!
Wicked men and liars have attacked me.
They tell lies about me,
and they say evil things about me,
attacking me for no reason.
They oppose me, even though I love them
and have prayed for them.
They pay me back evil for good
and hatred for love.

But, Lord my God, help me as you have
    promised,
and rescue me because of the goodness of your
    love.
I am poor and needy;
I am hurt to the depths of my heart.
Like an evening shadow I am about to vanish;
I am blown away like an insect.
My knees are weak from lack of food;
I am nothing but skin and bones.
When people see me, they laugh at me;
they shake their heads in scorn.

Help me, O Lord my God;
because of your constant love, save me!
I will give loud thanks to the Lord;
I will praise him in the assembly of the people,
because he defends the poor man
and saves him from those who condemn him to
    death.

Glory to the Father, and to the Son, and to the
    Holy Spirit:
as it was in the beginning, is now, and will be for
    ever. Amen.

Prayer
O God,
you punished Judas for his crime
and rewarded the good thief for his faith.
As our Lord Jesus Christ in his passion
gave to each according to his deserts,

so may we be given the grace
to rise again with him,
freed from our former sin and error.
We ask this through Christ our Lord.
Amen.

A Reading from the Acts of the Apostles (1:16–19)

Peter stood up to speak. "My brothers," he said,
"the Scripture had to come true in which the Holy
Spirit, speaking through David, made a prediction
about Judas, who was the guide for those who
arrested Jesus. Judas was a member of our group,
for he had been chosen to have a part in our
work." With the money that Judas got for his evil
act he bought a field, where he fell to his death;
he burst open and all his insides spilled out. All
the people in Jerusalem heard about it, and so in
their language they call that field Akeldama,
which means "Field of Blood."

Responsory

May his house become empty; may no one live
    in it.
*May his house become empty; may no one live
    in it.*
May someone else take his place of service.
*May his house become empty; may no one live
    in it.*
Glory to the Father, and to the Son, and to the
    Holy Spirit.
*May his house become empty; may no one live
    in it.*

A Reading from the Good News according to St. Mark (14:43–46, 50)

Jesus was still speaking when Judas, one of the twelve disciples, arrived. With him was a crowd armed with swords and clubs and sent by the chief priests, the teachers of the Law and the elders. The traitor had given the crowd a signal: "The man I kiss is the one you want. Arrest him and take him away under guard." As soon as Judas arrived, he went up to Jesus and said, "Teacher!" and kissed him. So they arrested Jesus and held him tight. Then all the disciples left him and ran away.

Do you think that I will not drink the cup of suffering.
Which my Father has given me?

Canticle of Joel (2:1–2, 11, 13)
*Antiphon: How terrible for the one who betrays
the Son of Man.*

Blow the trumpet;
sound the alarm on Zion,
God's sacred hill.

Tremble, people of Judah!
The day of the Lord is coming soon.
It will be a dark and gloomy day,
a black and cloudy day.
How terrible the day of the Lord!
Who will survive it?

Come back to the Lord your God.
He is kind and full of mercy;
he is patient and keeps his promise;
he is always ready to forgive
and not to punish.

Glory to the Father, and to the Son, and to the
 Holy Spirit:
as it was in the beginning, is now, and will be for
 ever. Amen.

Prayer
Father,
look with love upon your people,
the love which our Lord Jesus Christ showed us
when he delivered himself to evil men
and suffered the agony of the cross,
for he lives and reigns with you and the Holy
 Spirit,
one God, for ever and ever.
Amen.

Blessing
May Christ Jesus, betrayed even by his friends,
† bless us and keep us.
Amen.

DAY 22

Peter Denies Jesus

Simon Peter had confessed Jesus as Messiah and Lord; at the Supper he had promised fidelity "even if I have to die with you"; but in the courtyard of the high priest, he quails before a serving girl, protesting that he does not even know "the man."

Come, let us worship Christ our Savior.
He was betrayed into the hands of sinners.

Psalm 140: Jesus Prays as His Disciples Desert Him
Antiphon: Hear my cry for help, Lord!

Save me, Lord, from evil men;
keep me safe from violent men.
They are always plotting evil,
always stirring up quarrels.
Their tongues are like deadly snakes;
their words are like cobra's poison.

Protect me, Lord, from the power of the wicked;
keep me safe from violent men
who plot my downfall.

Proud men have set a trap for me;
they have laid their snares,
and along the path they have set traps
to catch me.

I say to the Lord, "You are my God."
Hear my cry for help, Lord!
Lord, my God, my strong defender,
you have protected me in battle.
Lord, don't give the wicked what they want;
don't let their plots succeed.

Lord, I know that you defend the cause of the
    poor
and the rights of the needy.
The righteous will praise you indeed;
they will live in your presence.

Glory to the Father, and to the Son, and to the
    Holy Spirit:
as it was in the beginning, is now, and will be for
    ever. Amen.

Prayer
Heavenly Father,
protector of those who trust in you,
rescue us from lying lips and a deceitful heart,
and teach us to confide in you alone;
through Christ our Lord.
Amen.

A Reading from the First Letter of Peter the Apostle (3:21–25)

Christ himself suffered for you and left you an example, so that you would follow in his steps. He committed no sin, and no one ever heard a lie come from his lips. When he was insulted, he did not answer back with an insult; when he suffered, he did not threaten, but placed his hopes in God, the righteous Judge. Christ himself carried our sins in his body to the cross, so that we might die to sin and live for righteousness. It is by his wounds that you have been healed. You were like sheep that had lost their way, but now you have been brought back to follow the Shepherd and Keeper of your souls.

Responsory

Christ died for our sins once and for all.
Christ died for our sins once and for all.
A good man on behalf of sinners.
Christ died for our sins once and for all.
Glory to the Father, and to the Son, and to the
    Holy Spirit.
Christ died for our sins once and for all.

A Reading from the Good News according to St. Matthew (26:31–35)

Jesus said to his disciples, "This very night all of you will run away and leave me, for the scripture says, 'God will kill the shepherd, and the sheep of the flock will be scattered.' But after I am raised to life, I will go to Galilee ahead of you." Peter spoke up and said to Jesus, "I will never leave you, even though all the rest do!" Jesus said to Peter, "I tell you that before the rooster crows tonight, you will say three times that you do not know me." Peter answered, "I will never do that, even if I have to die with you!" And all the other disciples said the same thing.

The Lord turned around and looked straight at Peter.
Peter went out and wept bitterly.

Canticle: O Savior of the World

Lord Jesus, Savior of the world,
    stir up your strength and help us.

By your cross and your precious blood,
    you have redeemed us,
    save us and help us.

You saved your disciples
    as they were on the point of perishing,
    hear us and save us.

In your great mercy,
    loose us from our sins,
    we humbly pray.

Reveal yourself as our savior and mighty deliverer,
    that we may praise you.

Come again and dwell with us,
    Lord Jesus Christ,
    and stay with us for ever.

And when you return in glory,
    may we share the life of your blessed
    kingdom.

Thanks be to God.
    Amen, amen!

Prayer
Almighty God,
whose glory is always to have mercy:
Be gracious to all who have gone astray from your
        ways,
and bring them again with penitent hearts and
        steadfast faith
to embrace and hold fast the unchangeable truth
        of your Word,
Jesus Christ, your Son,
who with you and the Holy Spirit lives and reigns,
one God, for ever and ever.
Amen.

Blessing
May Christ Jesus, betrayed into the hands of
sinners,
† bless us and keep us.
Amen.

DAY 23

Jesus Is Scourged and Crowned with Thorns

Betrayed by one disciple, denied by another, abandoned by all, Jesus is condemned by the elders of his people and handed over to Pontius Pilate to be stripped of his human dignity and prepared for the ultimate sacrifice.

Come, let us worship Christ, our Lord and Savior.
He bore our sins in his own body.

Psalm 13: Jesus Cries Out to His Father
Antiphon: Pilate handed Jesus over to them to be crucified.

How much longer will you forget me, Lord?
Forever?
How much longer will you hide yourself from me?
How long must I endure trouble?
How long will sorrow fill my heart day and night?
How long will my enemies triumph over me?

Look at me, O Lord my God,
and answer me.

Restore my strength;
don't let me die.
Don't let my enemies say,
"We have defeated him."
Don't let them gloat over my downfall.

I rely on your constant love;
I will be glad because you will rescue me.
I will sing to you, O Lord,
because you have been good to me.

Glory to the Father, and to the Son, and to the
    Holy Spirit:
as it was in the beginning, is now, and will be for
    ever. Amen.

Prayer
Lord Jesus Christ, suffering servant of God,
you were unjustly condemned to death,
mocked, scourged, and crowned with thorns,
pierced by nails and scorned by unbelievers.
By your holy and glorious wounds,
guard and keep us from all evil
and bring us to the victory you have won for us.
You live and reign for ever and ever.
Amen.

A Reading from the Prophet Isaiah (50:5–8)

The Lord has given me understanding, and I have
not rebelled or turned away from him. I bared my
back to those who beat me. I did not stop them
when they insulted me, when they pulled out the

hairs of my beard and spit in my face. But their insults cannot hurt me because the Sovereign Lord gives me help. I brace myself to endure them. I know that I will not be disgraced, for God is near, and he will prove me innocent.

Responsory
Because of our sins he was wounded.
Because of our sins he was wounded.
Beaten because of the evil we did.
Because of our sins he was wounded.
Glory to the Father, and to the Son, and to the
   Holy Spirit.
Because of our sins he was wounded.

A Reading from the Good News according to St. Mark (15:15–20)
Pilate wanted to please the crowd, so he set Barabbas free for them. Then he had Jesus whipped and handed him over to be crucified. The soldiers took Jesus inside to the courtyard of the governor's palace and called together the rest of the company. They put a purple robe on Jesus, made a crown out of thorny branches, and put it on his head. Then they began to salute him: "Long live the King of the Jews!" They beat him over the head with a stick, spat on him, fell on their knees, and bowed down to him. When they had finished making fun of him, they took off the purple robe and put his own clothes back on him. Then they led him out to crucify him.

He was so disfigured.
That he hardly looked human.

Canticle of Isaiah (12:2–6)
Antiphon: My spirit rejoices in God my Savior.

Surely, it is God who saves me;
I will trust in him and not be afraid.
For the Lord is my stronghold and my sure
    defense,
and he will be my Savior.
Therefore you shall draw water with rejoicing
from the springs of salvation.
And on that day you shall say,
Give thanks to the Lord and call upon his Name;
Make his deeds known among the peoples;
see that they remember that his Name is exalted.
Sing the praises of the Lord, for he has done great
    things,
and this is known in all the world.
Cry aloud, inhabitants of Zion, ring out your joy,
for the great one in the midst of you is the Holy
    One of Israel.

Glory to the Father, and to the Son, and to the
    Holy Spirit:
as it was in the beginning, is now, and will be for
    ever. Amen.

Prayer

Lord Jesus Christ,
you came among us first
as the suffering servant of God.
When you come again in glory
to judge the living and the dead,
be our peace and our salvation,
for you have redeemed us with your precious
    blood.
You live and reign for ever and ever.
Amen.

Blessing

By his holy and glorious wounds, may Christ our
    Lord
† guard us and keep us.
Amen.

DAY 24

The Way of the Cross

The disciples have fled, the crowds have clamored for his death, the Roman governor has pronounced sentence. As Jesus is led out to "the Place of the Skull" only the Daughters of Jerusalem are capable of compassion.

Come, let us worship Christ, our Lord and Master.
He carried the cross for our salvation.

Psalm 35: Jesus Appeals for Vindication Against His Foes

Antiphon: Carrying his own cross, Jesus went out to the Place of the Skull, where they crucified him.

O Lord, plead my cause against my foes;
fight those who fight me.
Take up your buckler and shield;
arise to help me.

Take up the javelin and the spear
against those who pursue me.

O Lord, say to my soul:
"I am your salvation."

Lying witnesses arise
and accuse me unjustly.
They repay me evil for good:
my soul is forlorn.

Now that I am in trouble they gather,
they gather and mock me.
They take me by surprise and strike me
and tear me to pieces.

O Lord, how long will you look on?
Come to my rescue!
Do not let my lying foes
rejoice over me.

Vindicate me, O Lord, in your justice,
do not let them rejoice.
Do not let them think: "Yes! we have won,
we have brought him to an end."

Glory to the Father, and to the Son, and to the
     Holy Spirit:
as it was in the beginning, is now, and will be for
     ever. Amen.

Prayer

Lord Jesus Christ,
you were led out to die on the cross
for the salvation of the world.
We ask your forgiveness for the sins of the past
and your protection from all future evil.
Bring us to the peace and joy of that kingdom
where you live and reign for ever and ever.
Amen.

A Reading from the Prophet Isaiah (52:14; 53:2, 8)

Many people were shocked when they saw him;
he was so disfigured that he hardly looked human.
He had no dignity or beauty to make us take
notice of him. There was nothing attractive about
him, nothing that would draw us to him. He was
arrested and sentenced and led off to die, and no
one cared about his fate.

Responsory

Holy is God, holy and strong, holy and living for
ever.
*Holy is God, holy and strong, holy and living for
ever.*
By the power of the holy cross, save us from sin
and death.
*Holy is God, holy and strong, holy and living for
ever.*
Glory to the Father, and to the Son, and to the
Holy Spirit.

Holy is God, holy and strong, holy and living for ever.

A Reading from the Good News according to St. Luke (23:26–31)

When they led Jesus forth, they requisitioned on the way one Simon of Cyrene, who was just returning from the country, and put the cross on him to carry it behind Jesus. A great multitude of the people accompanied him, notably women who bewailed and lamented him. Turning to them, Jesus said: "Daughters of Jerusalem, do not weep for me; weep for yourselves and your children; for mark my words, a time is coming when people will say, 'How blessed the barren are! How blessed the wombs that have never borne children, and the breasts that have never nursed!' Then they will actually cry out to the mountains, 'Fall upon us!' and to the hills, 'Bury us!' Yes, if this is done to the green wood, what must be the fate of the dry?"

Surely he has borne our griefs and carried our sorrow.
The Lord laid on him the iniquity of us all.

Canticle

King, high exalted,
all the world's Redeemer,
to you your children
lift their eyes with weeping;

Christ, we implore you,
hear our supplications.

Right hand of the Godhead,
headstone of the corner,
path of salvation,
gate to heaven's kingdom,
cleanse your sinful people
stained with transgressions.

On our knees before you,
Majesty eternal,
we lament our sinfulness
in your holy hearing.

Humbly now confessing,
countless sins admitting,
we lay bare our secrets:
may your boundless mercy
grant to us full pardon.

Captive led away,
guiltless, unresisting,
charged by false witness,
unto death for sinners,
Jesus Christ protect us
whom your blood has purchased.

Attende Domine

Prayer
Almighty God,
whose most dear Son
went not up to joy before first he suffered pain,

and entered not into glory before he was
  crucified,
mercifully grant that we, walking in the way of the
  cross,
may find it none other than the way of life and
  peace;
through Jesus Christ your Son our Lord,
who lives and reigns with you and the Holy Spirit,
one God, for ever and ever.
Amen.

Blessing
May the glorious passion of our Lord Jesus Christ
† bring us to the joys of paradise.
Amen.

DAY 25

Jesus Is Nailed to the Cross

"Because of a tree, Adam and Eve were estranged from Paradise; because of the Tree, the thief came to dwell in Paradise; by tasting of the tree, the former disobeyed the command of the Creator; but the latter, who was crucified with you, confessed you as the hidden Lord of all. O Savior, remember him and us in your kingdom" (Byzantine Liturgy).

Come, let us adore Christ, the Son of God.
He was lifted up on the cross for our salvation.

Psalm 22: Jesus' Cry of Anguish
Antiphon: They tear at my hands and feet. All my bones can be seen.

My God, my God, why have you abandoned me?
I have cried desperately for help,
but still it does not come.
During the day I call to you, my God,
but you do not answer;
I call at night,
but get no rest.

But you are enthroned as the Holy One,
the one whom Israel praises.
Our ancestors put their trust in you;
they trusted you, and you saved them.
They called to you and escaped from danger;
they trusted you and were not disappointed.

But I am no longer a man; I am a worm,
despised and scorned by everyone!
All who see me make fun of me;
they stick out their tongues
and shake their heads.
"You relied on the Lord," they say.
"Why doesn't he save you?
If the Lord likes you,
why doesn't he help you?"

Many enemies surround me like bulls;
they are all around me,
like fierce bulls from the land of Bashan.
They open their mouths like lions,
roaring and tearing at me.

My strength is gone,
gone like water spilled on the ground.
All my bones are out of joint;
my heart is like melted wax.
My throat is as dry as dust,
and my tongue sticks to the roof of my mouth.
You have left me for dead in the dust.

A gang of evil men is around me;
like a pack of dogs they close in on me;
they tear at my hands and feet.
All my bones can be seen.
My enemies look at me and stare.
They gamble for my clothes
and divide them among themselves.

O Lord, don't stay away from me!
Come quickly to my rescue!
Save me from the sword;
save my life from these dogs.
Rescue me from these lions;
I am helpless before these wild bulls.
I will tell my people what you have done;
I will praise you in their assembly.

Glory to the Father, and to the Son, and to the
    Holy Spirit:
as it was in the beginning, is now, and will be for
    ever. Amen.

Prayer
Lord Jesus Christ, Son of the living God,
set your passion, your cross and your death
between your judgment and our souls,
now and in the hour of our death.
In your goodness,
grant mercy and grace to the living
and forgiveness and rest to the dead;

to the Church and nation peace and concord;
and to us sinners life and glory without end.
You live and reign for ever and ever.
Amen.

A Reading from the Prophet Isaiah (53:4–6)
God's servant endured the suffering that should
have been ours, the pain that we should have
borne. Because of our sins he was wounded,
beaten because of the evil we did. We are healed
by the punishment he suffered, made whole by
the blows he received. All of us were like sheep
that were lost, each of us going his own way. But
the Lord made the punishment fall on him, the
punishment all of us deserved.

Responsory
We adore your cross, O Lord, and we praise and
    glorify your holy resurrection.
We adore your cross, O Lord, and we praise and
    glorify your holy resurrection.
For by the wood of the cross, joy came into the
    whole world,
We adore your cross, O Lord, and we praise and
    glorify your holy resurrection.
Glory to the Father, and to the Son, and to the
    Holy Spirit:
We adore your cross, O Lord, and we praise and
    glorify your holy resurrection.

A Reading from the Good News according to St. Mark (15:22–32)

They took Jesus to a place called Golgotha, which means "The Place of the Skull." There they tried to give him wine mixed with a drug called myrrh, but Jesus would not drink it. Then they crucified him and divided his clothes among themselves, throwing dice to see who would get which piece of clothing. It was nine o'clock in the morning when they crucified him. The notice of the accusation against him said: "The King of the Jews." They also crucified two bandits with Jesus, one on his right and the other on the left. People passing by shook their heads and hurled insults at Jesus . . . and the two who were crucified with Jesus insulted him also.

Look and see, all you who pass by.
See if there is any sorrow like my sorrow.

Canticle of the Cross

Moses prefigured the saving power of the cross,
when he lifted up his staff and split the Red Sea in
    two,
rescuing Israel on that day from the hand of
    Pharaoh (Ex 14).

Moses prefigured the saving power of the cross,
when he cast a tree into Marah's bitter waters,
making them fresh and sweet for a thirsty people
    (Ex 15).

Moses prefigured the saving power of the cross,
when Israel hardened its heart at Meribah
and put God to the test at Massah in the desert.
He struck the rock at Horeb with his staff
and brought forth living waters to quench their
thirst (Ex 17).

Moses prefigured the saving power of the cross,
when he extended his arms in the form of a cross
and defeated haughty Amalek in the desert of
Sinai (Ex 17).

Moses prefigured the saving power of the cross,
when he laid twelve staffs down before the Lord
in the tent of the commandments,
and Aaron's staff sprouted leaves, blossoms and
ripe almonds (Num 17).

Moses prefigured the saving power of the cross,
when he made a serpent of bronze
and mounted it on a pole in the desert;
all who looked at it with faith
recovered from the serpents' sting (Num 21).

Prayer
O Son of God and Savior of the world,
all these symbols now attain their perfection
and find their completion before our very eyes.
Reign from the noble tree of the cross
and establish the kingdom of God in our hearts.
You live and reign for ever and ever.
Amen.

Blessing
May the glorious passion of our Lord Jesus Christ
+ bring us to the joys of paradise.
Amen.

DAY 26

Jesus Dies on the Cross

"You were crucified, O Christ, for my sake that you might pour forth salvation for me. Your side was pierced with a spear that it might flow forth rivers of life for me. You delivered up your soul to your Father to bring me to Paradise with you. Glory to your blessed Passion, O life-giving Savior" (Byzantine Liturgy).

Come, let us adore Christ, the Son of God.
He redeemed us by his blood.

Psalm 141: Jesus Calls Out to His Father
*Antiphon: In the cross is victory; in the cross is
power.*

I call to you, Lord; help me now!
Listen to me when I call to you.
Receive my prayer as incense,
my uplifted hands as an evening sacrifice.

Lord, place a guard at my mouth,
a sentry at the door of my lips.

Keep me from wanting to do wrong
and from joining evil men in their wickedness.
May I never take part in their feasts.

A good man may punish me and rebuke me in
kindness,
but I will never accept honor from evil men,
because I am always praying against their evil
deeds.

When their rulers are thrown down from rocky
cliffs,
the people will admit that my words were true.
Like wood that is split and chopped into bits,
so their bones are scattered at the edge of the
grave.

But I keep trusting in you, Lord my God.
I seek your protection; don't let me die!
Protect me from the traps they have set for me,
from the snares of those evildoers.

Glory to the Father, and to the Son, and to the
Holy Spirit:
as it was in the beginning, is now, and will be for
ever. Amen.

Prayer
Merciful Father,
look upon this family of yours
for which our Lord Jesus Christ
did not hesitate to hand himself over to sinners

and to undergo the torment of the cross;
he now lives and reigns with you and the Holy
    Spirit,
one God, for ever and ever.
Amen.

A Reading from the First Letter of Peter the Apostle (2:21–25)

Christ suffered for you and left you an example, so that you would follow in his steps. He committed no sin, and no one ever heard a lie come from his lips. When he was insulted, he did not answer back with an insult; when he suffered, he did not threaten, but placed his hopes in God, the righteous Judge. Christ himself carried our sins in his body to the cross, so that we might die to sin and live for righteousness. It is by his wounds that you have been healed. You were like sheep that had lost their way, but now you have been brought back to follow the Shepherd and Keeper of your souls.

Responsory

We adore you, O Christ, and we bless you.
We adore you, O Christ, and we bless you.
For by your holy cross you have redeemed the
    world.
We adore you, O Christ, and we bless you.
Glory to the Father, and to the Son, and to the
    Holy Spirit.
We adore you, O Christ, and we bless you.

A Reading from the Good News according to St. Mark (15:33–39)

At noon the whole country was covered with darkness, which lasted for three hours. At three o'clock Jesus cried out with a loud shout, "Eloi, Eloi, lema sabacthani?" which means, "My God, my God, why did you abandon me?" Some of the people there heard him and said, "Listen, he is calling for Elijah!" One of them ran up with a sponge, soaked it in cheap wine, and put it on the end of a stick. Then he held it up to Jesus' lips and said, "Wait! Let us see if Elijah is coming to bring him down from the cross!" With a loud cry Jesus died. The curtain hanging in the Temple was torn in two, from top to bottom. The army officer who was standing there in front of the cross saw how Jesus had died. "This man was really the Son of God!" he said.

Jesus cried out in a loud voice.
Father, into your hands I place my spirit!

Canticle (Phil 2:5–11)
Antiphon: Christ is victor, Christ is ruler, Christ is Lord of all!

Though God by nature,
Jesus did not parade his equality with God
but despoiled himself of divine privilege
and became as we are.

149

An ordinary man to all appearances,
he stooped still lower yet,
even to the point of accepting death,
death on a cross.

That is why God has raised him so high
and conferred on him the most potent name of all.
At Jesus' name everyone in heaven, on earth and
    in hell
should bow adoring and should publicly
    proclaim,
to the glory of God the Father:
Jesus Christ is Lord!

Glory to the Father, and to the Son, and to the
    Holy Spirit:
as it was in the beginning, is now, and will be for
    ever. Amen.

Prayer
Lord Jesus Christ,
as you were expiring in agony at midafternoon,
you promised paradise to the repentant thief,
handed over your spirit to your Father
and descended among the imprisoned spirits
to enlighten and save them.
By the blood and water that flowed from your
    pierced side,
wash away all our sins,
renew in us a true and life-giving Spirit
and bring us to the resurrection of the body
and life everlasting in the world to come,

where you live and reign with the Father and the
    Holy Spirit,
one God, for ever and ever.
Amen.

Blessing
May the trophy of the life-giving cross
† deliver us from all sin and danger.
Amen.

DAY 27

Jesus Is Laid in the Grave

Jesus really died and was buried in a stone-cold tomb. But in the spirit he descended among the dead and brought life to those in the grave.

Come, let us adore Christ the Lord.
He was crucified, died and was buried for us.

Psalm 142: Jesus Prays To Be Delivered out of Death
Antiphon: Even in the valley of the shadow of death, you are with me.

I call to the Lord for help;
I plead with him.
I bring him all my complaints;
I tell him all my troubles.
When I am ready to give up,
he knows what I should do.
In the path where I walk,
my enemies have hidden a trap for me.
When I look beside me,
I see that there is no one to help me,

no one to protect me.
No one cares for me.

Lord, I cry to you for help;
you, Lord, are my protector;
you are all I want in this life.
Listen to my cry for help,
for I am sunk in despair.
Save me from my enemies;
they are too strong for me.
Set me free from my distress;
then in the assembly of your people
I will praise you,
because of your goodness to me.

Glory to the Father, and to the Son, and to the
    Holy Spirit:
as it was in the beginning, is now, and will be for
    ever. Amen.

Prayer
All-powerful and ever-living God,
your only Son went down among the dead
and rose again in glory.
In your goodness
raise up your faithful people,
buried with him in baptism,
to be one with him
in the eternal life of heaven,
where he lives and reigns with you and the Holy
    Spirit,
one God, for ever and ever.
Amen.

A Reading from the Prophet Isaiah (53:7–9)

He was treated harshly but he endured it humbly; he never said a word. Like a lamb about to be slaughtered, like a sheep about to be sheared, he never said a word. He was arrested and sentenced and led off to die, and no one cared about his fate. He was put to death for the sins of our people. He was placed in a grave with evil men, he was buried with the rich, even though he had never committed a crime or ever told a lie.

Responsory

Christ died for sins once for all to lead us to God.
Christ died for sins once for all to lead us to God.
And in the spirit went to preach to the spirits in
    prison.
Christ died for sins once for all to lead us to God.
Glory to the Father, and to the Son, and to the
    Holy Spirit.
Christ died for sins once for all to lead us to God.

A Reading from the Good News according to St. Mark (15:42–47)

It was toward evening when Joseph of Arimathea arrived. He was a respected member of the council, who was waiting for the coming of the Kingdom of God. It was Preparation Day (that is, the day before the Sabbath), so Joseph went boldly into the presence of Pilate and asked him for the body of Jesus. Pilate was surprised to hear that Jesus was already dead. He called the army officer and asked him if Jesus had been dead a long time. After hearing the officer's report, Pilate told Joseph he could have the body. Joseph bought a linen sheet, took the body down, wrapped it in the sheet, and placed it in a tomb which had been dug out of solid rock. Then he rolled a large stone across the entrance to the tomb. Mary Magdalene and Mary the mother of Joseph were watching and saw where the body of Jesus was placed.

I was dead but now I am alive for ever.
I hold the keys of death and of hell.

Canticle of Jonah (2:2–9)
Antiphon: Salvation comes from the Lord!

In my distress, O Lord, I called to you, and you
    answered me.
From deep in the world of the dead
I cried for help, and you heard me.
You threw me down into the depths,
to the very bottom of the sea,
where the waters were all around me,
and all your mighty waves rolled over me.

I thought I had been banished from your presence
and would never see your holy Temple again.
The water came over me and choked me;
the sea covered me completely,
and seaweed wrapped around my head.
I went down to the very roots of the mountains,
into the land where gates lock shut for ever.

But you, O Lord my God,
brought me back from the depths alive.
When I felt my life slipping away,
then, O Lord, I prayed to you,
and in your holy Temple you heard me.

Glory to the Father, and to the Son, and to the
    Holy Spirit:
as it was in the beginning, is now, and will be for
    ever. Amen.

Prayer

O God, Creator of heaven and earth:
Grant that, as the crucified body of your dear Son
was laid in the tomb and rested on the holy
    Sabbath,
so we may await with him the coming of the third
    day,
and rise with him to newness of life;
who now lives and reigns with you and the Holy
    Spirit,
one God, for ever and ever.
Amen.

Blessing

May Christ who holds the keys of life and death
† bless us and keep us.
Amen.

DAY 28

Christ Rises from the Tomb

Christ is risen! He is risen indeed! Alleluia! "We are Easter people and alleluia is our song" (St. Augustine).

Christ is risen, alleluia!
Come, let us adore him, alleluia!

Hymn
Who is this who comes to us in triumph,
Clothed in royal garments dyed with blood,
Walking in the greatness of his glory,
Bearing in his hand the holy rood?

This is Christ the risen Lord, the Strong One,
He who trod the winepress all alone;
Out of death he comes with life unending,
Seeking those he purchased for his own.

Great and wonderful is our Redeemer,
Christ the Living One, the just and true.
Praise him with the Father and the Spirit,
Ever with us, making all things new.

Based on Isaiah 63:1–7

Psalm 118: Christ Declares the Rescuing Power of God

Antiphon: Alleluia, alleluia, alleluia!

Give thanks to the Lord for he is good;
  his loving-kindness endures forever.

The right hand of the Lord has triumphed!
The right hand of the Lord is exalted!
The right hand of the Lord is victorious!

I shall not die but live,
  to declare the deeds of the Lord.
He has given me a sore punishment,
  but he has not handed me over to death.

Open to me the gates of victory,
  that I may enter and give thanks to the Lord.

  "This is the gate of the Lord;
  the righteous may enter it."

I thank you because you answered me;
  and you have become my salvation.

  "The stone that the builders rejected
  has become the chief cornerstone."

This is the Lord's doing;
  it is marvelous in our sight.

"This is the day when the Lord has acted;
let us rejoice and be glad in it!"

Hosanna! Hosanna!
Save us, Lord, and prosper us, we pray.

"Blessed is he who comes in the Name of the
Lord;
we bless you from the house of the Lord."

Give thanks to the Lord for he is good;
his loving-kindness endures forever.

Glory to the Father, and to the Son, and to the
Holy Spirit:
as it was in the beginning, is now, and will be for
ever. Amen.

Prayer
Lord Jesus Christ,
by your cross and resurrection,
you destroyed death
and brought life to those in the grave.
May your blessed passion be the joy of the whole
world
and may the glory of your rising from the tomb
ever be our song,
O Savior of the world,
living and reigning with the Father and the Holy
Spirit,
now and for ever.
Amen.

A Reading from the First Letter of Paul the Apostle to the Corinthians (15:1–7)
I passed on to you what I had received, which is of the greatest importance: that Christ died for our sins, as written in the Scriptures; that he was buried and that he was raised to life three days later, as written in the Scriptures; that he appeared to Peter and then to all twelve apostles. Then he appeared to more than five hundred of his followers at once, most of whom are still alive, although some have died. Then he appeared to James, and afterwards to all the apostles.

Easter Sequence
O flock of Christ, your homage bring
To Christ the Lamb, your glorious King!
His Easter praise in triumph sing!
Alleluia, alleluia, alleluia!

Peace has come down from God on high!
The King of peace in death did lie!
To save the sheep the Lamb did die!

Never on earth was stranger sight:
Life fought with death in darkest night,
Yet lives to reign in endless light!

What saw you, Mary, on your way?
"I saw the tomb where Life once lay,
Whose glory shone this Easter Day!

Angels their joyful tidings spread!
Grave-clothes I saw where none lay dead,
The cloth that once had veiled his head!

Christ is my hope, who rose for me!
Soon will you all his glory see!
Christ bids you go to Galilee!"

Christ has indeed aris'n again
As Lord of life, to rule all men!
On us have mercy, Lord! Amen.
Alleluia, alleluia, alleluia!

Victimae Paschali Laudes

A Reading from the Good News according to St. Mark (16:1–8)

After the Sabbath was over, Mary Magdalene, Mary the mother of James, and Salome brought spices to go and anoint the body of Jesus. Very early on Sunday morning, at sunrise, they went to the tomb. On the way they said to one another, "Who will roll away the stone for us from the entrance to the tomb?" (It was a very large stone.) Then they looked up and saw that the stone had already been rolled back. So they entered the tomb, where they saw a young man sitting at the right, wearing a white robe—and they were alarmed. "Don't be alarmed," he said. "I know you are looking for Jesus of Nazareth, who was crucified. He is not here—he has been raised! Look, here is the place where he was placed.

Now go and give this message to his disciples,
including Peter: 'He is going to Galilee ahead of
you; there you will see him, just as he told you.' "

This is the day that the Lord has made, alleluia!
Now let us be glad and rejoice, alleluia!

Easter Anthem—Christ Our Passover
(1 Cor 5:7–8; Rom 6:9–11; 1 Cor 15:20–22)
Alleluia.
Christ our Passover has been sacrificed for us;
    therefore let us keep the feast,
Not with the old leaven, the leaven of malice and
        evil,
    but with the unleavened bread of sincerity and
        truth.
    Alleluia.

Christ being raised from the dead will never die
        again;
    death no longer has dominion over him.
The death that he died, he died to sin, once for
        all;
    but the life he lives, he lives to God.
So also consider yourselves dead to sin,
    and alive to God in Jesus Christ our Lord.
    Alleluia.

Christ has been raised from the dead,
    the first fruits of those who have fallen asleep.

For since by a man came death,
  by a man has come also the resurrection of the
    dead.
For as in Adam all die,
  so also in Christ shall all be made alive.
    Alleluia.

Prayer

Almighty and ever-living God,
you sealed a covenant of reconciliation with us
in the mystery of Christ's passing from death to
    life.
May we come to everlasting joy
by a holy keeping of these Easter festivities.
We ask this through Christ our risen Lord.
Amen.

Blessing

Let us bless the Lord, alleluia, alleluia!
And give him thanks, alleluia, alleluia!
May Christ our Passover
† bless us and keep us.
Amen.

DAY 29

Christ Ascends into Heaven

Jesus returns to his Father in triumph. The Lord Jesus is the King of Glory, the Life of the new creation, the Giver of the Spirit, the Sovereign of the cosmos.

Come, let us worship Christ the Lord, alleluia!
As he ascends into heaven, alleluia!

Psalm 24: Christ's Triumphant Entry into Heaven
Antiphon: He ascended into heaven and is seated at the right hand of the Father.

Fling wide the gates,
open the ancient doors,
and the king of glory will enter in!

Who is this great king of glory?

He is the Lord Christ, strong and mighty,
the Lord Jesus, victorious in battle.

Fling wide the gates,
open the ancient doors,
and the king of glory will enter in!

Who is this great king of glory?

He is the Lord Christ, strong and mighty,
The Lord Jesus, victorious in battle.

Fling wide the gates,
open the ancient doors,
and the king of glory will enter in!

Who is this great king of glory?

The Lord of the heavenly armies,
he is the great king of glory!

Glory to the Father, and to the Son, and to the
    Holy Spirit:
as it was in the beginning, is now, and will be for
    ever. Amen.

Prayer
God our Father,
make us joyful in the ascension of your Son Jesus
    Christ.
May we follow him into the new creation,
for his ascension is our glory and our hope.
We ask this through the same Christ our Lord.
Amen.

A Reading from the Letter of Paul the Apostle to the Colossians (3:1–4)

You have been raised to life with Christ, so set your hearts on the things that are in heaven, where Christ sits on his throne at the right side of God. Keep your minds fixed on things there, not on things here on earth. For you have died, and your life is hidden with Christ in God. Your real life is Christ and when he appears, then you too will appear with him and share his glory!

Responsory

Christ went up, above and beyond the heavens, alleluia!

Christ went up, above and beyond the heavens, alleluia!

To fill the whole universe with his presence, alleluia!

Christ went up, above and beyond the heavens, alleluia!

Glory to the Father, and to the Son, and to the Holy Spirit.

Christ went up, above and beyond the heavens, alleluia!

A Reading from the Good News according to St. Luke (24:50–53)

Jesus led his disciples out of the city as far as Bethany, where he raised his hands and blessed them. As he was blessing them, he departed from them and was taken up into heaven. They worshipped him and went back into Jerusalem,

filled with great joy, and spent all their time in the
Temple giving thanks to God.

I ascend to my Father and to your Father, alleluia!
To my God and to your God, alleluia!

A Pauline Canticle (1 Tim 3:16)
*Antiphon: Praise the Lord, all you nations! Praise
          him, all you peoples!*

Jesus Christ appeared in human form,
was shown to be right by the Spirit,
and was seen by angels.

He was preached among the nations,
was believed in the world,
and was taken up to heaven.

He is the blessed and only Ruler,
the King of kings and the Lord of lords,
he alone is immortal.

Glory to the Father, and to the Son, and to the
      Holy Spirit:
as it was in the beginning, is now, and will be for
      ever. Amen.

Prayer
O King of glory and Lord of hosts,
who ascended triumphantly above the heavens:
do not leave us orphans,

but send us the Promised of the Father,
the Spirit of truth.
You live and reign for ever and ever.
Amen.

Blessing
May the King of glory, sitting at the right hand of
    the Father,
✝ bless us and keep us.
Amen.

DAY 30

Christ Sends Forth His Spirit

As the disciples of Jesus await his glorious return, his outpoured Spirit will teach them all they need to know and strengthen them in all their trials.

The Spirit of the Lord fills the whole, alleluia!
Come, let us adore him, alleluia!

Hymn to the Holy Spirit
O Holy Spirit, by whose breath
   Life rises vibrant out of death:
   Come to create, renew, inspire;
   Come, kindle in our hearts your fire.

You are the seeker's sure resource,
   Of burning love the living source,
   Protector in the midst of strife,
   The giver and the Lord of life.

In you God's energy is shown,
   To us your varied gifts made known.
   Teach us to speak, teach us to hear;
   Yours is the tongue and yours the ear.

Flood our dull senses with your light;
In mutual love our hearts unite.
Your power the whole creation fills;
Confirm our weak, uncertain wills.

From inner strife grant us release;
Turn nations to the ways of peace,
To fuller life your people bring
That as one body we may sing:

Praise to the Father, Christ his Word,
And to the Spirit, God the Lord;
To them all honor, glory be
Both now and for eternity.
Amen.

Veni, Creator Spiritus

Psalm 104: The New Creation

*Antiphon: When you give them breath, they live;
you give new life to the earth, alleluia.*

Praise the Lord my soul!
Lord, my God, how great you are!
You are clothed with majesty and glory,
you cover yourself with light.
You stretched out the heavens like a tent,
and built your home on the waters above.
You use the clouds as your chariot,
and walk on the wings of the wind.
You use the winds as your messengers,
and flashes of lightning as your servants.

From heaven you send rain on the mountains,
    and the earth is filled with your blessings.
You make grass grow for the cattle,
    and plants for us to use,
so we can grow our crops,
    and produce wine to make us happy,
olive oil to make us cheerful,
    and bread to give us strength.

Lord, you have made so many things!
    How wisely you made them all!
    The earth is filled with your creatures.
All of them depend on you,
    to give them food when they need it.
You give it to them, and they eat it;
    you provide food, and they are satisfied.
When you turn away, they are afraid;
    when you hold back your breath, they die,
    and go back to the soil they came from.

But when you give them breath, they live;
    you give new life to the earth.
May the glory of the Lord last forever!
    May the Lord be happy with what he made!
I will sing to the Lord all my life;
    I will sing praises to my God as long as I live.

Glory to the Father, and to the Son, and to the
        Holy Spirit:
as it was in the beginning, is now, and will be for
        ever. Amen.

Prayer

O God, on the first Pentecost,
you instructed the hearts of those who believed in
you
by the light of the Holy Spirit;
under the inspiration of the same Spirit
give us a taste for what is right and true
and a continuing sense of his joy-bringing
presence and power.
We ask this through Jesus Christ our Lord.
Amen.

**A Reading from the Acts of the Apostles
(2:17–19; cf. Joel 2:28–32)**

This is what I will do in the last days, God says:
I will pour out my Spirit on everyone.
Your sons and daughters will proclaim my
message;
Your young men will see visions,
and your old men will have dreams.
Yes, even on my servants, both men and women,
I will pour out my Spirit in those days,
and they will proclaim my message.
I will perform miracles in the sky above
and wonders on the earth below.

Responsory

Come, Holy Spirit, fill the hearts of your faithful.
Come, Holy Spirit, fill the hearts of your faithful.
And kindle in them the fire of your love.
Come, Holy Spirit, fill the hearts of your faithful.

Glory to the Father, and to the Son, and to the
Holy Spirit.
Come, Holy Spirit, fill the hearts of your faithful.

A Reading from the Good News according to St. John (14:16–17)

I will ask the Father, and he will give you another
Helper, who will stay with you forever. He is the
Spirit, who reveals the truth about God. The world
cannot receive him, because it cannot see or
know him. But you know him, because he
remains with you and is in you. When the Spirit
comes, who reveals the truth about God, he will
lead you into all truth.

The Helper, the Holy Spirit.
Will teach you everything.

Sequence of Pentecost

Holy Spirit, font of light,
   focus of God's glory bright,
   shed on us a shining ray.
Father of the fatherless,
   giver of gifts limitless,
   come and touch our hearts today.

Source of strength and sure relief,
   comforter in time of grief,
   enter in and be our guest.
On our journey grant us aid,
   freshening breeze and cooling shade,
   in our labor inward rest.

Enter each aspiring heart,
   occupy its inmost part
   with your dazzling purity.
All that gives to human worth,
   all that benefits the earth,
   you bring to maturity.

With your soft refreshing rains
   break our drought, remove our stains;
   bind up all our injuries.
Shake with rushing wind our will;
   melt with fire our icy chill;
   bring to light our perjuries.

As your promise we believe
   make us ready to receive
   gifts from your unbounded store.
Grant enabling energy,
   courage in adversity,
   joys that last for evermore.

Veni Sancte Spiritus

Prayer
Heavenly King, Consoler, Spirit of truth,
present in all places, filling all things,
treasury of blessings and giver of life:
Come and dwell in us,
cleanse us from every stain of sin
and save our souls,

O gracious Lord,
living and reigning with the eternal Father
and his only-begotten and beloved Son,
one Holy Trinity, now and for ever.
Amen.

Blessing
May the blessing of almighty God, the Father,
† the Son and the Holy Spirit, descend upon us
and remain with us for ever.
Amen.

DAY 31

Jesus Comes Again in Glory

The Kingdom of God begun in the person of Jesus continues in the Church, "Jesus become a people." It awaits in hope the Signs of the Times.

Come, let us adore Christ our Lord, alleluia!
He will come again in glory, alleluia!

Psalm 98: Come, Lord Jesus!
Antiphon: Blessed is he who comes in the name of the Lord.

Sing a new song to the Lord;
he has done wonderful things!
By his own power and holy strength
he has won the victory.

The Lord announced his victory;
he made his saving power known to the nations.
He kept his promise to the people of Israel
with loyalty and constant love for them.
All people everywhere
have seen the victory of our God.

Sing for joy to the Lord, all the earth;
praise him with songs and shouts of joy.
Sing praises to the Lord!
Play music on the harps!
Blow trumpets and horns,
and shout for joy to the Lord, our king.

Roar, sea, and every creature in you;
sing, earth, and all who live on you!
Clap your hands, you rivers;
you hills, sing together with joy before the Lord,
because he comes to rule the earth.
He will rule the peoples of the world
with justice and fairness.

Glory to the Father, and to the Son, and to the
    Holy Spirit:
as it was in the beginning, is now, and will be for
    ever. Amen.

Prayer
Remember your Church, O Lord,
deliver it from all evil,
and perfect it in your love;
make it holy
and gather it together from the four winds
into the kingdom prepared for it;
for yours is the power and the glory
for ever and ever.
Amen.

A Reading from the Letter of James (5:7–8, 9)

Be patient until the Lord comes. See how patient a farmer is as he waits for his land to produce precious crops. He waits patiently for the autumn and spring rains. You also must be patient. Keep your hopes high, for the day of the Lord's coming is near. The Judge is near, ready to appear.

Responsory

The kingdom of God is near at hand!
The kingdom of God is near at hand!
Turn away from your sins and believe the Good
    News.
The kingdom of God is near at hand!
Glory to the Father, and to the Son, and to the
    Holy Spirit.
The kingdom of God is near at hand!

A Reading from the Good News according to St. Mark (13:24–27, 33)

In the days after that time of trouble the sun will grow dark, the moon will no longer shine, the stars will fall from heaven, and the powers in space will be driven from their courses. Then the Son of Man will appear, coming in the clouds with great power and glory. He will send the angels out to the four corners of the earth to gather God's chosen people from one end of the world to the other. Be on the watch, be alert, for you do not know when the time will come.

The sign of the Son of Man will appear in the sky.
At a time when you are not expecting him.

Canticle of Habakkuk (3:2–6)

*Antiphon: I am coming soon, says the Lord.
Amen! Come, Lord Jesus!*

O Lord, I have heard what you have done,
and I am filled with awe.
Now do again in our times
the great deeds you used to do.
Be merciful, even when you are angry.

God is coming again from Edom;
the holy God is coming from the hills of Paran.
His splendor covers the heavens,
and the earth is full of his praise.
He comes with the brightness of lightning;
light flashes from his hand,
there where his power is hidden.
He sends disease before him
and commands death to follow him.

When he stops, the earth shakes;
at his glance the nations tremble.
The eternal mountains are shattered;
the everlasting hills sink down,
the hills where he walked in ancient times.

Glory to the Father, and to the Son, and to the
    Holy Spirit:
as it was in the beginning, is now, and will be for
    ever. Amen.

Prayer

Almighty God,
give us grace to cast away the works of darkness
and put on the armor of light,
now in the time of this mortal life
in which your Son Jesus Christ
came to visit us in great humility;
that on the last day,
when he shall come again in his glorious majesty
to judge both the living and the dead,
we may rise to the life immortal;
through him who lives and reigns with you and
    the Holy Spirit,
one God, now and for ever.
Amen.

Blessing

May almighty God, the Father, the Son and the
    Holy Spirit,
† bless us and keep us.
Amen.

Te Deum

You are God: we praise you;
You are the Lord: we acclaim you;
You are the eternal Father:
All creation worships you.

To you all angels, all the powers of
     heaven,
Cherubim and Seraphim, sing in
     endless praise:
   Holy, holy, holy Lord, God of
     power and might, heaven and
     earth are full of your glory.

The glorious company of apostles
     praise you.
The noble fellowship of prophets
     praise you.
The white-robed army of martyrs
     praise you.

Throughout the world the holy Church
     acclaims you:
   Father, of majesty unbounded,
your true and only Son, worthy of all
     worship,
   and the Holy Spirit, advocate and
     guide.

You, Christ, are the king of glory,
the eternal Son of the Father.

When you became man to set us free
you did not spurn the Virgin's womb.

You overcame the sting of death,
and opened the kingdom of heaven to
all believers.

You are seated at God's right hand in
glory.
We believe that you will come, and
be our judge.

Come then, Lord, and help your
people,
bought with the price of your own
blood,
and bring us with your saints
to glory everlasting.